Eccentric character : 27, 33, 34, 43-4,

Wives, marriages : 24, 30-1, 34,

Peasant : 19-20
life

Strengths, illness, medicine : 25^1

Debauchery : 25^2, 26, 28-9,

Streltsi : 30-31

When Peter the Great became undisputed Tsar of Russia in 1696, he was best known to his people as leader of the Drunken Association of Fools, a gang of young hooligans who terrorized the innocent citizens of Moscow. How could such a wild young man have the slightest idea how to govern the vast yet still barbaric state of seventeenth-century Russia? Yet thirty years later, when Peter died, he was remembered as the best and strongest Tsar that Russia had known, who had single-handed made his country the equal of the Great Powers of western Europe.

Michael Gibson shows how this young Romanov giant, nearly seven feet tall and immensely strong, needed a taste of power to bring out the best in him. He tells the fascinating story of how Peter visited Holland, France and England in disguise to see what Russia could learn from those nations. He explains how Peter threw himself wholeheartedly into all the business of state, personally chopping off the nobles' beards which he saw as a symbol of the old, backward Russia. At a more intimate level, he tells how this successful monarch was a tragic failure as a father.

Against a background of a crucial period in Russian and European history this book tells of a man who, in any country and at any time, would have been remarkable both in failure and in success, and who was justly called the Great.

Peter the Great

Michael Gibson

WAYLAND PUBLISHERS LONDON

More Wayland Kings and Queens

Alfred the Great	Jennifer Westwood
Henry VIII	David Fletcher
Mary Queen of Scots	Alan Bold
Elizabeth I	Alan Kendall
James I	David Walter
Charles I	Hugh Purcell
Charles II	Michael Gibson
Queen Victoria	Richard Garrett
Louis XIV	Christopher Martin
Napoleon I	Stephen Pratt
Charlemagne	Keith Ellis
Charles V	William Rayner
Wilhelm II	Richard Garrett
Peter the Great	Michael Gibson
Catherine the Great	Miriam Kochan

Frontispiece Peter the Great in armour, painted shortly after his great victory at the battle of Poltava.

SBN 85340 415 1
Copyright © 1975 by Wayland (Publishers) Ltd
101 Grays Inn Road London WC1
Printed by Page Bros (Norwich) Ltd, Norwich, England

Contents

1	The Rise of Russia	7
2	Neighbours and Enemies	10
3	Seventeenth Century Russia	15
4	The Young Tsar	21
5	The Great Embassy	27
6	The Lion of the North	37
7	St. Petersburg	41
8	The Battle of Poltava	47
9	Defeat on the Pruth	57
10	A Royal Tragedy	63
11	Peter's Triumph	69
12	Reform	75
13	Achievements of Peter the Great	82
	Table of Dates	90
	Principal Characters	93
	Further Reading	95
	Picture Credits	96
	Index	96

I The Rise of Russia

WHEN PETER THE GREAT became undisputed Tsar of Russia in 1696, he had little interest in governing the country. He enjoyed leading his army in battle, but otherwise his job did not seem a very exciting one. Peter much preferred to spend his time with his friends in the Drunken Association of Fools, wandering around Moscow terrorizing the peaceable citizens. He was soon to realize, though, that Russia had grave problems. Only a man with his strong personality could hope to tackle them. Peter never lost his taste for pleasure, and he always found it hard work to run the government, but when he died, thirty years later, he had done much to change Russia from a backward, ungovernable and barbaric state into a civilized and powerful country that was respected by its neighbours.

Russia's early history had been turbulent and bloody. The ancestors of the Russians, the Eastern Slavs, were driven into northern Europe by Attila and the Huns in the fifth century A.D. Their unruly tribes showed no signs of unity until after the arrival of the Varangian Vikings in the ninth century. These fierce warriors dominated the great trade routes running from the Baltic to the Black Sea and built fine cities like Kiev. In 988, two Greek monks, Cyril and Methodius, made their way to Russia and introduced Christianity. This was the beginning of Russia's cultural separation from Western Europe; the Greek Orthodox and the Roman Catholic Churches quarrelled and refused to have anything to do with each other.

Russia's isolation from Western Europe was com-

Below A fifteenth century *ikon* of the orthodox church, showing two martyrs.

Opposite Russian warriors of the twelfth century – Andrei Bogolyubski, Prince of Suzdal, leads an army against Novgorod.

Above left Ivan the Great, and *right*, Ivan the Terrible, the two Tsars responsible for Russia's rapid growth in the fifteenth and sixteenth centuries.

pleted by the Mongol invasions of the thirteenth century. For three hundred years, Russia was ruled by the mighty Khans of the Golden Horde. These Mongols had a deep and lasting influence upon the Russians. They taught them to accept the ideas of serfdom and all-powerful government.

During the Mongol period, the Princes of Moscow emerged from obscurity. In 1328, Prince Ivan Kalita or "Moneybags" persuaded the Mongol Khan to let him collect the tribute that was due from Muscovy to the Khans. From that day onwards, fighting sometimes for the Mongols and sometimes against them, the Princes of Moscow grew steadily in power and influence.

While Russia remained isolated, the rest of Europe was experiencing the Renaissance in the arts, the voyages of discovery, the Reformation and the scientific revolution. This great wave of change, which placed Western Europe in the forefront of world civilization for the next four hundred years, passed Russia by.

The true founder of modern Russia was Ivan the Great (1462–1505). He absorbed the tiny city-states of Yaroslavl, Ryazan, Rostov and Tver and created the state of Muscovy. Then, to strengthen his claims to pre-eminence, he married Zoe Palaeologus, the niece of the last Byzantine Emperor. As a result, in 1480, he declared that he was "by the grace of God, Tsar of all Russia." His gains were consolidated by his son, Vasily III (1505–33).

Further advances were made by Ivan the Terrible (1533–84). This strange and powerful man defeated the Mongols and seized their headquarters at Kazan and Astrakhan. Encouraged by these successes, Ivan hurled himself on Russia's old enemies, the Poles and Swedes. He had some success, but when he died it looked as if the state of Muscovy would collapse, as his heir, Fedor I (1584–98), was feeble-minded. But a remarkable man, half Russian and half Mongol, called Boris Godunov, seized control of the government and staved off a complete breakdown until 1605.

Then, between 1605 and 1613, Russia experienced "the Time of Troubles" when Polish and Swedish armies marched at will backwards and forwards across the country, looting and killing. At last, goaded beyond endurance by their enemies' brutality, the Russians rallied around Prince Pozharsky and drove the hated foreigners out of Russia.

As the old royal family had died out, the nobles or *Boyars* elected Michael Romanov (1613–45) as Tsar. They hoped that his sixteen year old boy would remain a puppet in their hands. As the years went by, though, Michael gradually threw off their influence and made himself the real ruler of Russia. His son, Alexis (1645–76), defeated both the Poles and a dangerous revolt of the Don Cossacks led by Stenka Razin. Alexis began to reorganize Russia's old-fashioned and inefficient government and army with the help of foreign experts.

Thus by the second half of the seventeenth century, Russia was on the way to becoming a powerful state. But could she produce a ruler great enough to build on these foundations?

Below Tsar Alexis Mikhailovitch, father of Peter the Great.

2 Neighbours and Enemies

Below Polish prisoners captured by Russian boyars in 1612. They were buried in sand, then beheaded with a scythe.

RUSSIA IN THE SEVENTEENTH CENTURY was much smaller than it is today. It stretched from the White Sea in the north to the Ukraine in the south, and from Lake Chudskoye in the west to the River Ural in the east. Its only harbour, Archangel on the White Sea, was frozen solid for half the year, so communication with the rest of Europe was not easy.

To the north-west of Russia lay the Baltic states with their rich ports of Riga and Reval. These were provinces of the great Swedish empire, as was Finland which lay further to the north. During the seventeenth century, Sweden's warrior kings made her the greatest power in the Baltic area. Her closest neighbour and bitterest rival was Denmark. The Danes had enjoyed great power and influence until they were eclipsed by the Swedes.

To the west lay Poland. Under the Jagellon kings during the Middle Ages, Poland had been a powerful state and had defended Europe against the attacks of the Ottoman Turks. But when the Jagellon family died out, they were succeeded by weaker men who failed to keep up Poland's position in Europe. Yet the Poles were still strong enough to put up a stiff struggle when the Russians tried to take over the Ukraine and its fierce inhabitants, the Cossacks. These people had been the vassals of the Poles since 1386, but as the years went by they became more and more friendly with the Russians. After a long and bitter struggle between 1654 and 1667, the Russians captured Smolensk and half the Cossack people. The Poles deeply resented this humiliating defeat and waited for a chance of revenge.

To the south lay the vast empire of the Ottoman Turks. These savage warriors captured Constantinople (the last relic of the Eastern Roman, or Byzantine, Empire) in 1453. By 1500 they had conquered Hungary, the Balkans, Asia Minor, most of the Middle East and the coast of North Africa. For many years, they hoped to add Western Europe to their empire, but were thwarted by the combined might of the Holy Roman Empire and Poland. On two occasions, in 1529 and 1683, they laid siege to Vienna, but were driven back by the Austrians. Denied further expansion in the west, they turned their attention to the north and made the Black Sea a Turkish lake. Here they fell foul of the Russians, who were hoping to expand into this area themselves. Ever since the fall of Constantinople, the

> "In no other country in the world is such drunkeness to be found . . . men, women, priests, laymen, roll about in the muddy streets and drink themselves to death."
> *A Serbian talking about Russia.*

Below Tsar Ivan the Terrible holds an enemy soldier's head on the end of his pike.

Below A Cossack horseman. The Cossacks fought on horseback with a spear and a dagger.

Russians had thought of themselves as the true heirs of the Byzantine Empire and dreamed of gaining control of the Bosphorus, the Sea of Marmora and the Dardanelles so that they could enter the Mediterranean Sea. As a result, this region was the scene of many fierce battles between the Russians and the Turks down to the twentieth century.

To the east lay the vast wilderness of the Steppes and Siberia, where a sparse population of nomads grazed their flocks and herds upon the rolling grasslands, a territory which stretched right across Asia to the Pacific ocean. The Russians were slow to recognize the economic value of this region. Not until the end of the sixteenth century did their farmers start to cultivate some of these rich prairies. There now began an epic struggle between the nomads and farmers for possession of this rich territory, which was not settled until the second half of the nineteenth century.

However, this northern world was something of a backwater compared with Western Europe, where a great struggle for power was taking place. For many years, Spain had dominated Western Europe, but after the death of Philip II in 1598, she had gone into rapid decline. However, her huge empire in South America was still the envy of every other European state. When it was learned that Charles II of Spain (1665–1700) would never have any children, the Western powers waited impatiently for him to die so that they could divide up his empire among themselves.

By far the most powerful of Charles' relatives was Louis XIV of France (1643–1715). Louis was a man of unbounded ambition, and hoped to prove his claim to most of the Spanish empire. The other great powers were just as determined to stop this happening, as it would make France far too strong. William of Orange, the ruler of both Britain and the United Provinces (present day Holland), put himself at the head of Louis' opponents with the powerful support of Leopold I, the Holy Roman Emperor. Western Europe was soon convulsed by a series of bloody wars: the War of

Devolution (1667–68), the Dutch War (1672–78), the Nine Years' War (1688–97) and the War of the Spanish Succession (1701–13). For this reason, the Western powers were not able to pay much attention to what was happening in northern Europe between 1667 and 1713.

Russia was thus perhaps better placed than ever before to strengthen her position in this area. Even so, she was still a poor, backward, weak country on the fringe of Europe, with little chance of sharing in the wealth and civilization of the west.

Above Louis XIV, the King of France who dominated Western Europe during the later seventeenth century.

> "Peter I, to police this nation, worked on it like aquafortis on iron." *Frederick the Great of Prussia, Memoirs.*

13

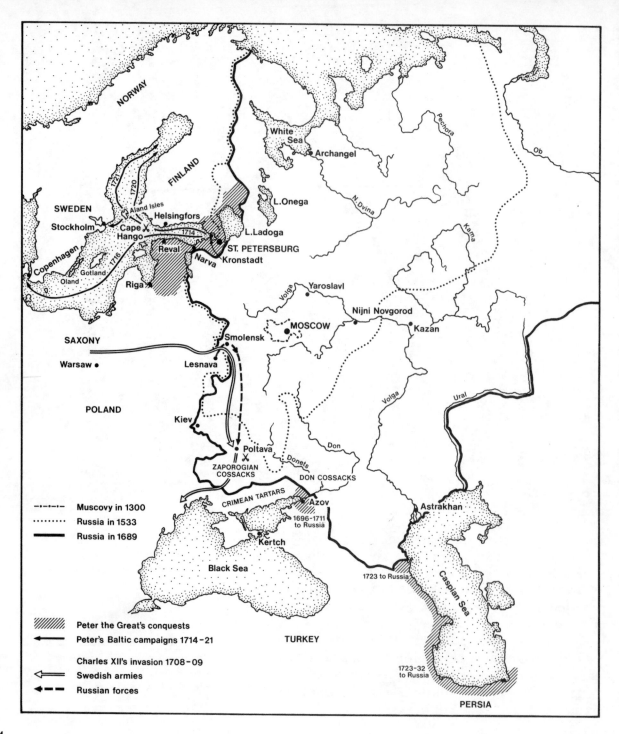

NORWAY

White Sea

Archangel

Pechora

Ob

FINLAND

L. Onega

N. Dvina

1721
1720

Aland Isles

SWEDEN

Helsingfors

Stockholm

Cape
Hango

1714

L. Ladoga

Reval

ST. PETERSBURG

Yaroslavl

Kazan

Copenhagen

Gotland

Narva

Kronstadt

Nijni Novgorod

Kama

1716

Oland

Riga

Volga

MOSCOW

Ural

SAXONY

Smolensk

Warsaw

Lesnava

POLAND

Kiev

Volga

Don

Poltava

Donets

ZAPOROGIAN
COSSACKS

DON COSSACKS

Astrakhan

CRIMEAN TARTARS

Azov

—·—·— Muscovy in 1300

.... Russia in 1533

1696–1711
to Russia

——— Russia in 1689

Kertch

1723 to Russia

Black Sea

Caspian Sea

TURKEY

1723–32
to Russia

Peter the Great's conquests

Peter's Baltic campaigns 1714–21

Charles XII's invasion 1708–09

Swedish armies

Russian forces

PERSIA

14

3 Seventeenth Century Russia

SEVENTEENTH CENTURY RUSSIA was ruled by an all-powerful autocrat, the Tsar. The Tsar's authority was unlimited. He could make laws and impose taxes whenever he liked. He could make the lowest of his subjects a lord, the highest a serf. He was commander-in-chief of the armed forces and head of the legal system. His very word was law. So great were his powers that only an exceptional man could hope to use them wisely, even with the help of skilful counsellors.

The central government was weak and inefficient. There were some forty *prikasy* or departments of state, whose duties often overlapped and conflicted with each other. Few civil servants could even read, and most were corrupt. Indeed, most of the Tsar's taxes found their way into their pockets instead of the Treasury. Not surprisingly, the Tsars were always short of money. Local government was in the hands of the sheriffs, who did much the same work as the Justices of the Peace in England. But because of Russia's vast size, the Tsar could not keep a close watch on all these local officials, and some of them became petty dictators in their own areas.

The Tsar had a standing army of twenty-two regiments each of a thousand men. These *Streltsy* or "Sharpshooters" were originally recruited from the people of Moscow and other leading towns, but by this time they had become a hereditary class. These soldiers were noted both for their pride and their special religious beliefs. They were never entirely trustworthy and several Tsars had to face dangerous

"The Tsar of Russia is an absolute monarch who does not have to answer for any of his actions to anyone in the world; but he has power and authority for the purpose of governing his states and lands according to his will and wise decision, as a Christian sovereign." *Peter the Great writing in 1716.*

Opposite Russia in the time of Peter the Great

Right Streltsy infantrymen of the seventeenth century. They carried muskets, but these were unreliable, and the axe was more useful for fighting at close quarters.

"They never learn any art or science or apply themselves to any kind of study; on the contrary they are so ignorant as to think that a man cannot make an almanack unless he be a sorcerer, not foretell the revolution of the Moon and the Eclipses, unless he have communication with Devils."
The Travels of Olearius, 1646.

Streltsy mutinies.

Every able-bodied man was expected to serve his country in time of war, but the Tsars preferred their professional troops, armed with musket and cannon, to the old feudal levies. However, as Russia was so woefully short of professional cavalrymen, the Tsar had to rely on squadrons of mounted gentry and nobility, whose enthusiasm far exceeded their skill.

Next in importance to the Tsar and his family were the princes, boyars and the new nobility. The princes and boyars were the descendants of local rulers and large landowners under the Mongols, whereas the new nobles had been given their titles by the Romanovs for their services to the royal family. The nobility of all kinds were forever fighting among themselves and plotting against the Tsars. Their selfishness and ignorance were formidable barriers to change and progress. Most of the leading nobility lived in and around Moscow. In peacetime, they attended the royal court and worked in the departments of state. In wartime, they formed the Tsar's bodyguard and served as officers in the other regiments. By the mid-seventeenth century the provincial nobility were also starting to move to the capital, in search of social advancement. Normally, however, they worked in the local government service, and spent most of their time on their own estates.

The nobility were divided into several classes enjoying very different standards of living. The Moscovite nobility lived in comparative luxury in their great town houses, while the provincial landowners lived much like their own peasants. The nobles, both high and low, were illiterate and barbaric in their manners. They spat, picked their noses and urinated in public. They had no interest in books, although they loved listening to poems and stories about great Russian heroes like Alexander Nevsky. Both men and women enjoyed the antics and coarse jests of itinerant clowns. The wives of the nobility were usually quiet and subdued in the presence of their husbands; wife-beating was a standard practice in seventeenth-century Russia. According to visitors from overseas, Russian women complained that their husbands did not love them if they were not beaten at least once a week.

Next to the nobility in status were the freemen of the towns. These merchants and traders were looked on with disdain by the proud boyars, but they were starting to make their mark. They earned a lot of money exporting flax, hemp, hides, wood, tar and pitch to Western Europe. They lived in simple wooden houses, which easily caught fire. Moscow was burned to the ground on many occasions during the Middle Ages.

Below Travel in Russia in winter. Most of the country is snow-covered for several months in the year.

Above A village of the Nogayan Tartars in the eighteenth century. They fitted wheels to their huts and moved around the plains in search of pasture for their animals.

Although the city streets were broad, they were unpaved and became rivers of mud during the winter, when pedestrians had to walk on specially raised sidewalks made of planks. The towns were full of inns and bath-houses where the Russians drank enormous quantities of vodka and beer. The Russians were very religious and there were almost as many churches as inns in every town. These magnificent buildings with their great domes and onion-shaped cupolas stood high above the surrounding houses and dominated the landscape. Inside, the air was filled with the smell of incense and the sound of chanting choirs. From the dimly-lit walls, the painted faces of countless saints peered down at the worshippers below.

Unfortunately, the Russians disagreed bitterly over

changes in liturgy and ritual and divided into "Old" and "New" Believers. The Old Believers were arch-conservatives who would not accept any changes in their religion or way of life. Indeed, between 1684 and 1690, more than twenty thousand of them burned themselves to death rather than conform. These Old Believers were another obstacle in the way of change.

At the bottom of the social scale were the peasants. Around 1600 there were many different kinds, ranging from slaves to small farmers, but during the next few years most of them became unfree "serfs" living in small villages belonging to the Tsar or the nobles. Their lives were spent in tilling the soil and raising stock. Their villages were surrounded by great open fields divided into strips. Each peasant worked a number of the strips in each field and grazed his cattle on the common ground. As the peasants knew nothing about fertilizers, they left one field fallow each year so that it could replace the food that the crops had absorbed from the soil in previous years. The peasants had to borrow each other's oxen to work their strips. In fact, they had to help each other all the time if they wanted to be successful farmers.

The peasants lived in small thatched wooden cottages. These hovels were divided by a thin partition into a living room where all the cooking and eating and much of the work was done, and a bedroom where the whole family slept, often in one big bed. Their only holidays were on Sundays and Saints' days, when they were expected to attend church. Their only amusements were singing, dancing, telling stories, playing games and getting thoroughly drunk.

The lives of the peasants were strictly regulated by their landlord, who insisted that they work on his land several days a week and pay him taxes in money and kind. Peasants were bought and sold like cattle. In 1721, the Tsar suggested that "the sale of single individuals should be stopped, or if this is impossible that they should be sold together with their families and households, not singly." However, this advice was

"If a man considers the natures and manner of the life of the Muscovites, he will be forced to allow there cannot be anything more barbarous than that people." *The Travels of Olearius, 1646.*

Above Russian peasant costumes—on the left, a seller of live fish. This was drawn for an English geography book in the eighteenth century.

"The peasants in Russia are in a state of abject slavery; and are reckoned the property of the nobles to whom they belong, as much as their dogs and horses. Indeed, the wealth of a great man in Russia is not computed by the extent of land he possesses, or by the quantity of grain he can bring to market, but by the number of his slaves. The owner has the power of selling his slave, or of hiring his labour to other persons." *William Richardson, an English visitor to Russia.*

ignored and many thousands of peasants were sold by their owners and separated from their wives, husbands or children. Many more were forced to fight in the armed forces, build towns and fortifications, or work in the new industries.

Landlords maintained control with the "knout," a particularly large and effective whip. Seventeenth century estate records are full of entries like this: "The offender is to be mercilessly beaten with the knout until there is scarcely any breath left in his body." The only way a peasant could escape from this life of drudgery was to run away and take refuge in the thinly-populated frontier areas in southern Russia and Siberia.

Even in the second half of the seventeenth century, the Russians were still illiterate, superstitious and opposed to change of any kind. Could anyone smash his way through these solid barriers of ignorance, bigotry and conservatism?

4 The Young Tsar

PETER THE GREAT WAS THE SON of Tsar Alexis and his second wife, Natalia Naryshkina. When Peter was born on 30th May 1672, nobody expected that he would become Tsar; Alexis already had two sons by his first marriage to Maria Miloslavsky. Indeed, when Alexis died in 1676, his eldest son, Fedor II, ascended the throne without opposition. Then, when Fedor died childless in 1682, the Naryshkin and Miloslavsky families struggled for power.

At first the Naryshkins got the upper hand and had the ten year old Peter elected Tsar. Not long afterwards, the Miloslavskys, led by Sophia, Tsar Alexis' eldest daughter, persuaded the Streltsy to rise in revolt and overthrow the Naryshkins. During the fighting, the boy Tsar had to stand by and watch several of his relatives being hacked to death. The triumphant Sophia did not dare to depose Peter, because of his popularity with the ordinary people, but she made her invalid brother, Ivan, co-Tsar.

For the next seven years, Sophia acted as regent for both boys. During this time, Peter's education was shamefully neglected. Natalia, his mother, took him to live in the village of Preobrazhensk just outside Moscow to keep him away from the spiteful Sophia. Peter was a headstrong boy who terrified his tutors with his violent temper and great physical strength. When he should have been studying, he was visiting the foreigners who lived in the so-called German suburb of Moscow. He persuaded these exiles to teach him foreign languages, mathematics and geography. However, he was not a very good scholar. His exercise books are full of spelling

Above The two sides of a medal struck to commemorate Peter's birth in 1672. The lower picture shows his parents, Alexis and Natalia.

Right Sophia Miloslavsky, Peter's half-sister, who acted as regent from 1682 to 1689.

mistakes and bad grammar.

His education was nothing like that normally given to the Tsars of Russia. No attempt was made to prepare him for his life as Tsar. He knew nothing about court life or the work of government. This was perhaps an advantage, as Peter grew up to be remarkably free from prejudice and was prepared to judge every situation on its merits. This partly explains why he was so different from the Tsars who came before and after him.

Peter was no intellectual, and much preferred working with his hands to thinking. By the time he was twelve, he was learning stonemasonry, carpentry, joinery and printing. Later on, he was to boast that he was skilled in fourteen different trades, including dentistry. During the course of his life, he slowly filled a sack with the teeth he had extracted! Although he could calculate the trajectory of a cannonball or the height of a wall, he despised all forms of literature, which he dismissed as "useless tales which merely waste time!" Stranger still, he disliked hunting and falconry, preferring to spend his spare time riding and walking.

Like most boys, he loved playing soldiers, and formed his friends into regiments. However, because he was co-Tsar of Russia, he was able to arm his "troops" with real muskets and cannon. In his mock battles, some of them were badly wounded or even killed. He had a real castle built beside a tributary of the Moscow River where he could practise siegecraft. Before long, these

Below Peter, aged about ten, giving orders to his friends as they play at being soldiers.

games became genuine manoeuvres, and Peter's boy soldiers became members of the famous Poteshnie regiment which fought in all his wars. Sometimes, Peter fought mock sea battles on Lake Voronezh, where he had some old boats refitted as miniature ships-of-the-line.

By the time he was seventeen, Natalia decided that he was old enough to get married and give Russia a male heir. Unfortunately, Peter had already fallen in love with a foreign girl called Anna Mons, who lived in the German Suburb. As a result, the wife whom his mother chose for him, a pretty girl called Eudoxia Lopukhina, never managed to win his love. Nevertheless, they were quite happy until Eudoxia gave birth to a son, christened Alexis, on 19th February 1690. After that Peter and Eudoxia quarrelled more and more, so that when their second child died shortly after birth, the Tsar refused to attend his funeral. Although Eudoxia remained his wife until 1707, it was in name only.

The Tsarevna Sophia clung to power even after her brother and half-brother reached manhood. In 1689, she decided to remove the threat to her position by having Peter murdered. But the young Tsar was warned in time and escaped wearing nothing but his nightshirt to the Troitsa monastery, where he was given sanctuary. The Muscovites threatened to overthrow Sophia when they learned of her treachery, and she lost her nerve and retired to the convent of Novodevich.

From that moment on, Peter and his half-brother Ivan were technically in charge of the government, but neither Peter who was too busy enjoying himself, nor Ivan who was too ill, took their duties seriously. As a result, Peter's mother, Natalia Naryshkina, was left in sole charge until 1695. In that year, the Turks declared war on Russia. Both the Turks and the Russians were determined to control the lands on the northern shore of the Black Sea. They had fought an earlier, indecisive war between 1676 and 1681. Now, the Turks saw a chance to strengthen their hold on the coastal provinces.

Peter saw how important this area was to Russia and threw himself into the war with tremendous enthusiasm. To the surprise of most of his subjects, he took personal command of the Russian army and laid siege to the great port of Azoff at the mouth of the River Don. However, between 8th July and 22nd September 1695, the Turks repulsed all the Russian attacks and forced them to withdraw. Peter realized that Azoff could not be taken without the aid of a fleet, so he had shipyards hastily built at Voronezh on the Don, with the help of some engineers sent by the Emperor Leopold. Europe was scoured for shipwrights and whole forests were felled to provide the timber for the new fleet. After a winter of superhuman effort, the ships were ready. Blockaded by land and sea, the Turks were forced to surrender on 29th July 1696. It was Peter's first taste of victory.

While the campaign was still in progress, first Peter's mother and then his half-brother died, leaving Peter in sole charge of Russia at the age of twenty-three. By this time, Peter was a giant, nearly seven feet tall, broad and immensely strong. He loved to show his strength by bending silver coins in half. However, in spite of his physical fitness, Peter suffered from a mysterious disease which caused violent muscular spasms. Because of the frequency and violence of these attacks, Peter was followed everywhere by a servant carrying his medicine, a mixture of ground magpies' wings and breasts. Moreover, he was subject to uncontrollable rages during which he attacked people with his fists, spat on them or thrashed them within an inch of their lives.

As a young man, he lived a wildly dissolute life, drinking heavily and womanizing. He was coarse in his habits, loving rough horseplay and unpleasant practical jokes. He liked nothing better than to make people eat and drink until they were violently sick. He himself seemed immune to the effects of heavy drinking and prided himself on being able to drink all his friends under the table.

> "A twitching of the face, not often occurring, but which appeared to contort his eyes and all his physiognomy and was frightful to see; it lasted a moment, gave him a wild and terrible air and passed away." *Saint Simon, the French diarist, writing about Peter.*

> "His Majesty's person was graceful, tall, and well made, clean and very plain in his apparel. He generally wore an English drab-colour clothfrock, never appearing in a dress suit of clothes, unless on great festivals, and remarkable holidays; on which occasions, he was sometimes dressed in laced clothes, of which sort he was not owner of above three or four suits." *John Bell, a Scotsman who served Peter as an engineer.*

25

B

Right Peter leads a procession in honour of Bacchus, the Greek god of wine, through the streets of Moscow.

Peter and his friends banded themselves together as the Drunken Association of Fools. Its first commandment was that members must never go to bed sober. They dressed up as priests and bishops, and held drunken services in which they poked fun at the elaborate rituals of the Church. They rode around on bullocks and asses, or had pigs, goats and bears pulling their sleighs. Sometimes, too, they parodied the court, with Peter dressing as a humble subject while a courtier played at being Tsar. The aim of the Association was to mock the pomposity and pretence of the court and the Church. Unfortunately, many of the ordinary people decided that Peter must be the Devil in human shape. Such beliefs landed them in the torture-chamber or on the scaffold.

Soon, the Tsar and his boon companions became the scourge of Moscow. Nobody was safe from them. How, the people asked themselves, could such a dissolute and flippant young man ever become a hardworking and successful Tsar?

5 The Great Embassy

NOW THAT HE WAS HIS OWN MASTER, Peter decided to tour Europe in search of experience. He was also looking for allies against the Turks. Most Russians were horrified, as they hated and feared the peoples of the west. Also the war with Turkey was still going on. Moreover, Peter insisted on going incognito, calling himself Peter Mikhailov. This scarcely fooled anyone, as he was accompanied by a "caravan" of thirty-two carriages and four wagons.

He set out on 31st March 1697, and made his way to Swedish Latvia. Once there, he fell out with the local governor because he claimed that the local people had put up their prices when he arrived. He then made his way to East Prussia, and spent a few enjoyable weeks with the Elector of Brandenburg. Then he moved to Holland, where he spent five months working in the famous Dutch shipyards as a carpenter. During this short time, Peter learned an amazing amount about shipbuilding and was able to make very good use of his newly-acquired knowledge when he came home to Russia.

In January, 1698, he crossed the Channel and landed in England, where huge crowds followed him wherever he went. Like any tourist, he visited all the places of interest in the London area including the Tower of London, Windsor Castle, Hampton Court and the Greenwich Observatory. After that, he spent some time at the naval dockyard at Deptford, studying English shipbuilding techniques. Then, to his joy, King William III gave him a magnificent yacht called *The Transport Royal*, and took him to watch the naval exercises on

"He often took the Carpenter's Tools in his Hands, and often work'd himself in Deptford Yard, as he had done in Holland. He would sometimes be at the Smith's, and sometimes at the Gun-founder's, and there was scarce any Art or mechanick Trade whatsoever, from the Watch-maker to the coffin-maker, but he more or less inspected it." *Captain John Perry, who visited Peter's empire, in his book The State of Russia.*

Above Peter learns the skills of carpentry in the shipyard at Saardam, in Holland.

"He left the country to deliver himself for a while from the crown, so as to learn ordinary life." *Napoleon Bonaparte on the Great Embassy.*

the Solent. The delighted Peter was heard to murmur that he would rather be an English admiral than the Tsar of Russia!

However, Peter's conduct in England did nothing to change peoples' view that he was an undisciplined barbarian. While he was staying at the house of the famous diarist, John Evelyn, he did £350 worth of damage. Not only did he steal some of the furniture and damage the staircase, but he amused himself by crashing backwards and forwards through Evelyn's prize hedges. The story was much the same at the inns where he and his suite stayed. The Russians ran up huge bills which they left the English Treasury to pay. At Godalming in Surrey, Peter and his companions ate "½ a hundredweight of beef, 1 sheep of equal weight,

¾ of a lamb, ½ a calf, 8 fowl, 8 rabbits" and drank "2½ dozen bottles of white wine and 1 dozen bottles of red wine" at one sitting.

On 9th May, Peter left England and went back to Amsterdam for a few days before going on to Vienna, where he hoped to persuade Emperor Leopold to join him in his war with the Turks. But Leopold refused even to consider such an idea. A disappointed Peter was about to leave for Venice, the great Mediterranean sea power, when he heard that the Streltsy, egged on by his half-sister Sophia, had risen in revolt. Peter had no choice but to cut short his tour and hurry back to Russia.

However, when he was only half-way home, he learned that General Schein had put down the mutiny, so he took the opportunity to visit the rulers through whose lands he was passing. As a result, he met Augustus the Strong, the new King of Poland, and discussed the idea of a war against Sweden. Not long afterwards, he reached Moscow and his great adventure was over.

How did the Great Embassy affect Peter's ways of thinking? On the whole it would be fair to say that it merely confirmed him in his previous beliefs. As he had expected, the Westerners proved to be far more advanced technologically than the Russians, so he lured at least two hundred master craftsmen to Russia by promises of high wages. He also sent more and more young Russians abroad to be educated in scientific and technical subjects.

The tour also widened Peter's own interests. He no longer confined himself to manual skills; he began to take a deep interest in science, biology, mineralogy and anatomy. However, in spite of his experiences, he remained remarkably blind to other aspects of Western life. For example, he paid little attention to Western political, financial and administrative institutions or to the arts. Indeed, Peter wasn't interested in understanding Western Europe; he simply thought that if Russia could acquire new technical skills, she would equal Britain and France in wealth and power.

"His journey is an epoch in the history, not only of his own country, but of ours and of the World." *Lord Macaulay, the nineteenth century historian.*

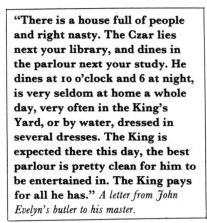

"There is a house full of people and right nasty. The Czar lies next your library, and dines in the parlour next your study. He dines at 10 o'clock and 6 at night, is very seldom at home a whole day, very often in the King's Yard, or by water, dressed in several dresses. The King is expected there this day, the best parlour is pretty clean for him to be entertained in. The King pays for all he has." *A letter from John Evelyn's butler to his master.*

Above Peter watches while his wife Eudoxia is whipped, in an attempt to make her confess that she had plotted against him.

On reaching Moscow, Peter set about finding out why the Streltsy had risen in revolt. In fact, they had many grievances. Even before Peter left on the Embassy, there had been many complaints about how many foreigners there were in the Russian army. Moreover, many of the Streltsy were Old Believers and hoped to reverse Peter's policy of supporting the New Believers. Then, while Peter was away on his tour, they were told that he had died, so they decided to overthrow the government and put their old ally, Sophia, on the throne.

Peter was determined to find incriminating evidence against his estranged wife, Eudoxia, and his half-sister Sophia. He set up fourteen torture-chambers in the capital and kept them busy night and day. Try as he

would, though, he could find nothing damning enough to warrant the executions of these two troublesome women. In a fury, Peter ordered the execution of all the mutineers. The Tsar took a vicious delight in personally slicing off the heads of these unfortunate men and insisted that his courtiers join him in his bloody work. No less than twelve hundred Streltsy were beheaded, broken on the wheel, or hanged. Throughout the winter, their frozen bodies were gruesomely displayed in front of the Kremlin and the convents where Eudoxia and Sophia had taken refuge.

To punish Eudoxia further, Peter took Alexis, his son, away from her and brought him up himself. Even though the young boy was extremely unhappy, Peter had no time to spare for him, so Alexis grew to hate

Above Peter takes his revenge on the rebellious Streltsy. Many were tortured before being hanged or beheaded.

"After torture came the executions. Finding the headsman too slow at his job, Peter picked up the axe himself and sent his subjects' heads rolling in the dust, a royal giant with contorted features, foam-flecked lips and clothes stained with his victims' blood."
Zinaida Schakovskoy, Precursors of Peter the Great.

32

and fear his father. Meanwhile, Eudoxia was forced to stay in her convent while Peter accused her of every crime under the sun. Sophia's convent was kept under close watch until she died a few years later. Peter's treatment of his relatives and the Streltsy show the black side of his character. He was a violent and cruel man who could not be trifled with.

As soon as the Streltsy had been taught their lesson, Peter introduced a host of unpopular reforms. His reasons for doing so at this time are hard to fathom. He certainly had no master plan for reorganizing Russia. The probable answer is that he decided to begin the mammoth task of breaking down the Russians' built-in conservatism. He started in dramatic fashion by rounding up Generals Schein and Romodanovsky and many of the leading nobles and having their beards shaved off. This was a serious matter, because the Russians believed that bearded men were made in the image of God and that beardless ones were no better than brute beasts. Indeed, there was such an outcry that Peter relented a little and allowed men to go on growing beards so long as they paid a heavy tax and wore a medal bearing the words, "Beards are ridiculous ornaments."

Next, he made everyone, except the clergy and farm labourers, wear short Hungarian-style clothes instead of long Russian robes. Once again, there was a certain amount of angry opposition, but whenever Peter saw anyone wearing Russian costume, he rushed over to him and cut off the bottom of his coat. In an effort to improve his nobles' manners, the Tsar published a book on etiquette which prohibited dancing in riding boots, spitting on floors, gnawing bones at meals and speaking with the mouth full. Moreover, he insisted that the nobles and their wives should come to court so that he could see that they behaved the way he told them to.

Peter was determined to do something about education, as very few Russians could read or write. There were few schools and even fewer teachers and textbooks. Indeed, when a School of Mathematics and

Above Peter displays the Hungarian-style clothes which he tried to make compulsory wear for his subjects.

"To shave the beard is a sin that the blood of all the martyrs cannot cleanse. Is it not to deface the image of God created by men?" *Ivan the Terrible.*

Opposite A contemporary cartoon shows Peter himself cutting off the beard of a Russian nobleman.

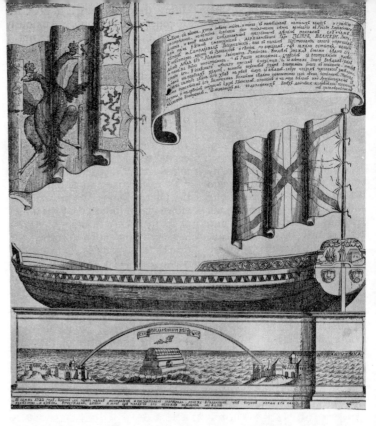

Naval Sciences was opened in 1701, its first principal found that hardly any of his pupils could read. As a result, Peter had the Russian alphabet simplified and encouraged the use of Arabic numerals; this made it much easier for the Russians to learn to read and calculate than before. Many European textbooks on technical subjects were translated into Russian and a number of high schools were founded. In an effort to persuade the young nobles to go to school, Peter announced that they would not be allowed to marry until they could read and write. Fortunately for them, it proved impossible to enforce this decree!

Next, he reformed the administration of the towns by replacing the unpopular sheriffs with elected burgesses. Then, he encouraged the growth of industries in Russia by providing would-be employers with capital and slave-workers. One result was the rise of a thriving armaments industry in the Urals.

Left Peter inspects his first fleet, at Voronezh, an inland port on the River Don.

His most successful reform was the reorganization of the armed forces. A Board of Admiralty was set up and a fleet of ships-of-the-line was built at Voronezh. Most of the vessels were very crude compared with those built by the Dutch and English, but a few, like *The Predestination*, designed by Peter himself, were fine ships by any standards. Then, in 1699, Peter raised a new army of thirty-thousand men by making every landlord provide a contingent from his estates. Since this force was mainly trained and officered by foreigners, it was very unpopular with the Russians. Peter did his best to overcome their objections by starting an officer training scheme for Russians; but they were slow to volunteer, and unwilling to study their profession.

Not all Peter's reforms derived from a desire to improve Russian efficiency, however. Some were frankly selfish. For example, he encouraged smoking, because he enjoyed it himself and because the tobacco industry was a state monopoly and earned large profits for the crown. Still, these early reforms did go some way towards weakening Russian conservatism and were an essential preparation for the deeper changes that were to be made later in the reign.

"His Majesty on this Occasion [the fall of Azoff in 1696] finding great Advantage of a Maritime Force declared to his Lords that he was resolved to establish a Navy on that Side, that he might maintain this important place [Azoff], and be able to meet the Turks and oppose them in the Black Sea, and commanded immediately to send for Builders and Artificers from Holland to build his ships, and from Italy and Venice to build his Galleys."
Captain John Perry, The State of Russia.

6 The Lion of the North

WHILE PETER WAS FORCING THROUGH HIS REFORMS, a situation arose in northern Europe which he could not afford to ignore. In 1697, a fifteen-year-old boy became King Charles XII of Sweden. Immediately, Denmark, Poland and Russia saw that they had a unique chance to attack and destroy Sweden's Baltic empire. However, Charles XII was ready for them. This strange young man loved war for its own sake. He lived like a common soldier, eating the plainest food, drinking only a little beer and wearing a private's uniform. When the allies declared war in 1790, he hurled himself against them and crushed them in a brilliant campaign.

The Russians had always wanted an outlet onto the Baltic coast. This was because the way out from the Black Sea was controlled by Turkey, while their northern ports were frozen up for most of the winter. It was thus impossible for Russia to develop any overseas trade. Peter had therefore led an army into Swedish Ingria, and was besieging the port of Narva. Suddenly, without warning, the Swedish King, who had swiftly beaten the Poles and the Danes, appeared before Narva at the head of his cavalry. Without waiting for his infantry and artillery to arrive, he hurled himself on the Russian positions and completely defeated them. Peter was astonished by the skill and courage of this brilliant teenager.

At this moment, Russia lay at Charles' feet. However, instead of marching on Moscow, as Peter gloomily predicted, Charles went back to Poland to strengthen his position there by placing his friend, Stanislas Lesczynski, on the throne. Peter could hardly believe

"Surely you have no doubt but that I with my 8,000 brave Swedes shall trample down 80,000 Russians." *Charles XII to his generals on the eve of the attack.*

Opposite Peter the Great in military uniform, painted by Franz Casanova, brother of the notorious adventurer.

Above A cartoon of a Cossack horseman, showing him loaded down with loot taken from the peasants whose villages they raided.

his luck, but made full use of this unexpected breathing space. He brought in conscription and set about forming a huge army. In a nation-wide effort to obtain

Left Charles XII of Sweden, aged 18.
He became a popular hero abroad
after his victory at Narva, and copies
of this engraving were being sold in
London in 1702.

enough metal for the armaments industry, the churches
and monasteries were stripped of their bells. These were
melted down and made into cannon. For the first time,
the Russians manufactured their own flintlock muskets:
6,000 a year in 1701, 40,000 by 1711.

The home-made Russian cannon turned out to be
very good indeed. An English officer serving with the
Russians wrote enthusiastically that he had "never
seen any nation do better work with their cannons and
mortars than the Russians." Thanks to the effectiveness
of these great guns, Peter's armies were able to force
the surrender of town after town in Ingria, Estonia and
Latvia while Charles XII was still kept busy by his

39

Above A medal struck to celebrate Peter's capture of Noteborg from the Swedes in 1702. Cannon, mortars, sailing ships and rowing boats are shown being used during the siege.

Polish campaigns.

However, the Russian cavalry remained a great problem. The Russian troopers became so excited in battle that they forgot their instructions and ran completely out of control. Peter tried to stop this by insisting that they should only be used as a shock weapon. They were ordered to charge the enemy at a full gallop with drawn swords. They were not allowed to use their pistols until they were engaged in hand-to-hand fighting.

These reforms made the Russian army a force to be reckoned with. Peter felt that his conquests were secure, and that the time had come for him to build a new capital facing the Baltic.

7 St. Petersburg

PETER WANTED HIS NEW CAPITAL to outshine the finest cities of Europe; but he chose an apparently uninviting site near the mouth of the River Neva in Ingria. Thousands of unfortunate peasants were formed into labour battalions and marched off to this desolate area where they froze in winter and baked in summer. During the years that followed, thousands of them died of malaria and malnutrition.

Peter persuaded architects and engineers from all over Europe to come and superintend the work in return for high salaries. Alexandre Leblond, Peter's chief architect, was paid 5,000 roubles a year (perhaps £40,000 or $100,000 in today's money). Nothing was too much trouble for the Tsar where St. Petersburg, as his new capital was called, was concerned. When the local stone quarries could no longer supply the builders with enough materials, Peter banned the use of building stone in the rest of the country so that every quarry could send its entire stock to the capital. Peter loved trees and imported five thousand limes, oaks, chestnuts, yews and maples from Holland for the new city. He was particularly fond of maples, and insisted that every street should be lined with them.

The Russian nobility were ordered to move their households from Moscow to St. Petersburg. But when they came to build their new homes, they found that their plans had to be approved by the Tsar's architects. Peter had a model house built to show everyone what he wanted. This can still be seen in Leningrad (as Peter's capital as been called since the Russian Revolu-

> "This is as it were, the bottomless pit in which innumerable Russian subjects perish and are destroyed."
> "A heap of villages linked together, like some plantation in the West Indies."
> "A wonder of the world, considering its magnificent palaces . . . and the short time that was employed in building it."
>
> *Anonymous Russians talking about St. Petersburg.*

41

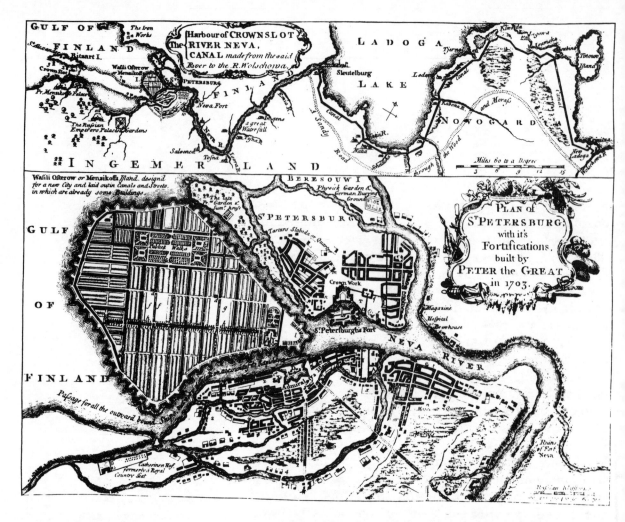

Above St. Petersburg, from a map drawn near the end of Peter's reign. The canal was later extended as far as Kronstadt (shown as Crownslot on the upper map).

tion of 1917). All this careful planning made St. Petersburg one of the most beautiful cities in the world, as indeed it is today.

Nor did Peter neglect the defences of the city. A grim fortress dedicated to St. Peter and St. Paul was built on an island in the middle of the River Neva so that it could dominate both the city and the river. At the mouth of the Neva he built the port of Kronstadt, which had its own shipyards and batteries of guns.

In spite of Peter's known wishes, the English and Dutch merchants went on trading at Archangel, be-

cause St. Petersburg could not be reached by water. To satisfy their needs Peter had the capital linked to the Gulf of Finland by canals. Then he forbade the sale of hemp, Russia's main export, in any other port but St. Petersburg, so that the foreign merchants had to buy their goods there whether they liked it or not.

When Peter stayed in St. Petersburg, he loved to live almost alone in a tiny four-roomed wooden house. The doorways were so low that he had to bend double as he moved from room to room. However, it was in this homely atmosphere that he worked out many of his plans for war or reforms. It was pleasant to escape from the hurly-burly of court life, but Peter realized that he still needed a magnificent palace just outside the city where he could receive ambassadors and visiting royalty. As a result, he employed a French architect to design him a palace like the one Louis XIV of France had built at Versailles. This beautiful palace, called the Peterhof, had splendid terraces, fountains, a cascade, a picture gallery and a magnificent park.

Nevertheless, Peter still hated court life. When he first became Tsar, he had sacked large numbers of servants

Above The workman's cottage in which Peter lived during the building of St Petersburg.

43

Above This drawing of the palace of the Tsars at St Petersburg was made in 1853, but the palace was largely unaltered since Peter's day.

and had been content with ten or twelve faithful retainers. As a result, the cost of the royal household had fallen from several hundred thousand roubles a year to a mere sixty thousand. Unlike most kings, Peter had hardly any silver and gold plate or state robes. He preferred to wear his comfortable old clothes even if they were covered in patches. On state occasions, he borrowed the necessary plate from his nobles!

Life at Peter's court was far different from the order and refinement that surrounded the French kings whose great palace he had imitated. His taste for crude practical jokes was indulged at the great state dinners which he had to give although he never enjoyed them. Dr. Birch, a visitor from England, described how Peter's cooks "often bake cats, wolves, ravens and the like, in their pastries, and when the company have eaten them up, they tell them what they have in their guts." To add to the fun, the Tsar made sure that there

44

were not enough seats for all his guests, so there was a mad scramble for places. Once a guest had found a place, he had to defend it by "cuffing and boxing" those who tried to take it from him. As a result of these disgraceful scenes, several foreign ministers refused to dine at court, much to the Tsar's amusement.

"As soon as one sits down," wrote Dr. Birch, "one is obliged to drink a cup of brandy, after which they ply you with great glasses of adulterated Tokay." This was followed by so many glasses of wine and beer that many of the guests were drunk before the soup arrived! Moreover, each guest had only one plate during dinner so he had to eat up every scrap of each course or mix the remains with his new food. Some guests shovelled their leftovers onto their neighbours' plates while they were not looking, then wiped their plates clean on the tablecloth.

Peter often became bored in the middle of these great feasts and strolled out to visit his friends in the town. Meanwhile, his courtiers went on with the festivities as if nothing had happened. Eventually, many hours later, Peter would come back and behave as if he had never been away. Nobody dared to leave the palace before he returned, because he was sure to notice and have them punished.

To please his second wife, Catherine, he gave grand balls and concerts, although he disliked both dancing and music. While the courtiers were dancing, he would sit in a corner with his cronies and play chess, smoke a pipe and drink beer. At other times, he would walk up and down the room with a glass of wine in his hand chatting cheerfully to everybody.

During the summer, Peter held fancy dress parties in a grove of oaks near his palace. The guests sat on wooden benches and drank neat vodka. Armed guards were posted all round the gardens to stop the courtiers slipping away as the vodka was replaced by corn brandy. As the night wore on, the Tsar became more and more excited. Sometimes, he climbed onto one of the tables and sang and danced. Often these parties went on for

"The company . . . make such a noise, racket, halloing, that it is impossible to hear one another, or even to hear the music, which is playing in the next room, consisting of a sort of trumpets and cornets, for the Tsar hates violins, and with his revelling noise and uproar the Tsar is extremely diverted, particularly if the guests fall to boxing and get bloody noses." *Dr. Birch, an English visitor at Peter's court.*

Above St. Petersburg grew rapidly during the eighteenth century. This drawing shows the quays on the River Neva shortly after Peter's death.

more than a week at a time. Peter would wander off to his yacht on the Neva for a few hour's sleep. When he came back, the drinking would still be going on.

However, under the influence of his second wife, Catherine, Peter finally agreed that some pomp and circumstance was necessary. He began to spend more and more money on his court and palaces. By the end of his reign, the Russian court was as lavish and colourful as it had been in the days of his predecessors. Even so, Peter still liked nothing better than to put on his old clothes and visit the building sites and docks of his beloved capital. Even in this attire, as the Tsar strode furiously through the streets it was easy enough to pick him out because of his great height and noble bearing. He was every inch a king.

8 The Battle of Poltava

IN 1708, THE YOUNG CHARLES XII turned his attention once more to Russia and crossed the River Vistula at the head of a magnificent army of 46,000 men. The Swedish King was brimming over with confidence for, as one of his generals commented, "He believes that he is the agent of God on earth." Charles now realized that his hold on Poland would never be secure until the Russians had been conquered.

Charles had chosen his time well. Russia was in a state of chaos. Peter's secret police informed him that Russians of every class were seething with discontent because of his high taxes and reforms. A series of peasant revolts culminated in 1707 with a great rising by the Don Cossacks led by Konrad Bulavin. The Cossacks carried fire and sword throughout southern Russia. Fortunately for Peter, the Russian nobility were so frightened by this threat to their lands that they forgot their own grievances and concentrated on destroying the rebels. Bulavin and his followers were trapped and butchered in the summer of 1708. All the same, this rising encouraged Charles XII to believe that the peasants would rise in his support if he invaded Russia.

For months, Charles had been in touch with Mazeppa, the cunning *Hetman* or commander of the Zaporogian Cossacks. These proud herders and stock-breeders prided themselves on their independence. For many years, they had fought for the Russians as mercenary troops. Indeed, they had played a key part in the capture of Azoff in 1696. During the Great Northern War, many of them served in the Russian army and were away from home for years at a time. While on

Left Peter leads a cavalry charge at the battle of Poltava, one of a series of mosaics celebrating the Russian victory.

"As for the cavalry, we are ashamed to look at them ourselves, let alone show them to the foreigner: sickly, ancient horses, blunt sabres, puny, badly dressed men who do not know how to wield their weapons. There are some noblemen who do not know how to charge the arquebus, let alone hit the target. They care nothing about killing the enemy, but think only how to return to their homes. They pray that God sends them a light wound so as not to suffer much, for which they will receive a reward from their sovereign. In battle they hide in thickets; whole companies take cover in a forest or a valley and I have even heard noblemen say 'Pray God we may serve our sovereign without drawing out our swords from their scabbards.'" *Peasant Pososhkov, a soldier in Peter's army.*

49

Right A symbolic print of 1714 showing
Alexander Menschikov being crowned
with a laurel wreath for his services to
Peter as a general and statesman.
Menschikov used his power to amass a
vast fortune from bribery.

campaign, they heard disturbing stories about the way
the Russians were treating their families back at home.
On hearing of their discontent, Charles approached
Mazeppa and offered to drive the Russians out of the
Ukraine if the Cossacks would help him conquer Russia.

At first, Mazeppa was sceptical and told Peter all about the plot, but at the beginning of 1708, he suddenly changed his mind and gave the Swedish King his support.

Unaware of Mazeppa's treachery, Peter ordered his armies to retreat before the Swedes, laying waste the land through which the enemy had to travel. Peter expected Charles to attack Novgorod and then make for Moscow or St. Petersburg, but Charles did nothing of the sort. He had worked out a daring plan. He would march south to the Ukraine and join up with Mazeppa's Cossacks before striking north-east towards Moscow. The success of this plan depended upon Charles being reinforced and re-equipped by a relief force under General Lewenhaupt. However, the Russians intercepted Lewenhaupt at Lesnaya on 9th October and forced him to destroy his precious baggage train. By the time the unlucky general reached Charles' camp he had only a tiny fragment of his original force left.

Charles had made a bad start, but worse was to follow. As soon as Peter learned of Mazeppa's treachery, he acted like lightning. General Menshikov was sent off to the Ukraine to capture Mazeppa's headquarters and destroy all his supplies and munitions. By the time Charles arrived, it was too late. The Cossacks were now unwilling to join him because he had failed to protect them from Peter, and all the roads to Moscow were blocked by Russian troops. Like it or not, the Swedish King had to spend the winter in the Ukraine.

As luck would have it, the winter of 1708–9 was the coldest in living memory, and the poorly-equipped Swedes suffered terribly. To stay alive, they had to force the unwilling Cossacks to share their dwindling supplies of food and fuel with them. By the end of the winter, the Cossacks hated the Swedes as much as they did the Russians, and refused to help them against Peter. Nevertheless, Peter was still worried that Charles might obtain help from the Turks, so he spent the winter refitting the Black Sea fleet at Voronezh and assembling a huge army outside Azoff. None of this

Below General Gordon, a Scotsman who, like others from many European countries, served as a mercenary in Peter's army.

Above A tapestry portrait, made in Paris, of Peter at the battle of Poltava – another example of how the Tsar's fame spread throughout Europe.

was lost on the Sultan, Ahmed III. This cautious man decided to sit back and watch the Swedes and Russians destroy each other. Then would be the time for him to invade Russia.

The Swedes were wholly cut off from home, and had

to live off the land they invaded. By the spring of 1709, they were starving and desperately short of ammunition, so Charles XII laid siege to the town of Poltava in the hope of obtaining supplies. Unfortunately for him, the town was well fortified and refused to surrender. While Charles waited impatiently for the citizens of Poltava to crack, Peter arrived at the head of eighty thousand men. The scene was set for one of the greatest battles in the world's history.

Only two days later, Charles was shot in the foot while reconnoitring the city's defences. Stubborn as always, he refused to have the wound dressed and carried on with his inspection until he collapsed through loss of blood. When his companions got him to his tent, they found that his foot was so badly smashed that they had to cut off his boot before the surgeons could get to work. Encouraged by this news, Peter advanced to attack the Swedish army.

Undismayed, Charles prepared to face his formidable opponent. He left two thousand men outside Poltava to stop the garrison breaking out and joining the Tsar. A further three and a half thousand were left to guard the Swedish baggage train. The remaining thirteen thousand made ready to do battle with the Russians. By this time, the Swedish infantry had only enough powder and shot left to fire one volley. After that they had to defend themselves as best they could with their swords and bayonets. The Swedish artillery could not be used at all. In normal circumstances, the Swedes would not have stood a chance, but as long as Charles XII was alive anything seemed possible.

Peter prepared his positions with care. The Russian army was deployed in a straight line between two woods on the west bank of the River Vorskla. Six gun emplacements were built in front of the line so that the Swedes would have to advance under heavy fire. Undeterred, Charles ordered the attack early on the morning of 28th June. The Swedes were drawn up in three columns. The centre was commanded by General Lewenhaupt, the left wing by General Sparre and the right by

"The infantry are armed with bad muskets and do not know how to use them. They fight with their side-arms, with lances and halberds, and even these are blunt; for every one foreigner killed there are three, four and even more Russians killed."
Peasant Pososhkov, a soldier in Peter's army.

53

General Roos. As Charles was still weak from loss of blood, he placed General Rehnskold in overall command. This was a mistake; the Swedish general was so used to taking orders that he was incapable of controlling the battle by himself.

The Swedes rushed into the attack with all their usual courage and determination. Ignoring terrifying casualties, the Swedish left wing swept past the redoubts facing them, and sword in hand, forced their way through the Russian lines on to the plain beyond. Peter was in despair and was ready to run away. Fortunately, before he could do so, he heard that the Swedish right wing had been defeated. The brave Roos had charged the two redoubts facing him three times and been bloodily repulsed on each occasion. Recovering quickly, Peter ordered General Menschikov to attack Roos with ten thousand troops. The luckless Swedes were surrounded and forced to surrender.

Meanwhile, in the centre, Lewenhaupt passed between the gun emplacements, smashed his way through the Russian lines and joined Sparre's left wing. All was not yet lost. Then the weakened Swedish army halted for just a moment to regroup for the final attack. During this short time, Peter was able to bring forward all his cannon so that when the Swedes launched their final charge, they were met with a hail of shot from a hundred cannon and forty thousand muskets. The advancing troops were cut to pieces and the battle was over.

When the fighting ended at midday, between three and four thousand Swedes had been killed or wounded and another two to three thousand captured. Lewenhaupt led the remaining twelve thousand southwards until they were surrounded and forced to surrender three days later. Charles XII and a few companions escaped and, in the confusion, managed to slip across the border into Turkey.

Apart from the momentary loss of courage at the start of the battle, Peter performed brilliantly. He was in the thick of the battle from start to finish, encouraging his men by word and deed. He was nearly killed three times. One bullet passed harmlessly through his hat, a second ricocheted off his saddle and a third hit and dented the cross he always wore around his neck. On the evening after the battle, Peter gave a dinner for the defeated Swedish generals. He and his officers stood and drank a toast to their gallant opponents. That night, Peter wrote triumphantly, "Now with God's help the last stone has been laid of the foundation of St. Petersburg."

The Poltava campaign was the greatest Peter ever fought. He was not a brilliant military commander, as he openly admitted; his strength lay in his ability to amass huge armies and to play a waiting game. Peter did not have Charles' genius for attack. He preferred to wait in well-fortified camps for his enemies' onslaught, hoping to triumph through sheer weight of numbers. His understanding of tactics was still poor, as he was to show on his next campaign against the Turks.

КОТЪ КАЗАНКОЙ АУМЪ
СТРАХАНКОЙ РАЗУМЪ
СИБИРСЮЙ СЛАВIЮ ЖИ
ЛЪ СЛАТКОЕЛЪ СЛАПКО
БЗДЕЛЪ

56

9 Defeat on the Pruth

WHILE THE RUSSIAN ARMIES were conquering Sweden's Baltic provinces between 1709 and 1713, Charles XII remained in Turkey, hoping to persuade the reluctant Sultan to declare war on Peter. At first, he had little success, but Peter had become over-confident after his victory at Poltava, and dreamed of creating a great southern empire by freeing the Christian Slavs of Moldavia and Wallachia (what is now Rumania) from Turkish rule.

With great recklessness, Peter provoked the powerful Sultan into declaring war. Confident in his own powers and those of his troops, Peter advanced rapidly along the west coast of the Black Sea, and greatly over-extended his lines of communication. Also the local people, although they hated their Turkish rulers, had no greater liking for the Russians, and did not give Peter the help he had hoped for. To his surprise, the Turks suddenly appeared in overwhelming force and surrounded his army at Stanileshte near the River Pruth. Charles XII was jubilant, believing that the Turks would avenge his defeat at Poltava. However, the Sultan did not realize how weak Peter really was, and agreed to a truce. As a result, Peter managed to talk himself out of a very tricky situation and obtain a generous treaty. True, he had to hand back all his conquests in southern Russia, including Azoff, to the Turks, but at least he was able to withdraw with his army intact.

This defeat clearly exposed Peter's limitations as a strategist and tactician. He underestimated the strength of his opponents throughout the campaign, and he

Opposite A contemporary Russian cartoon shows Peter as a wild cat with two tails, symbolizing his ferocity and duplicity. *See also pages 84–5.*

failed to protect his line of retreat. In the end he was lucky not to lose his whole force. Certainly, this defeat taught Peter a lesson he would never forget. In future, he planned his campaigns with much greater care and was far more cautious.

Meanwhile, Charles XII was still in Turkey trying to persuade the Sultan to follow up his victory by invading Russia. By 1713, the Sultan had had enough of his uninvited guest and ordered him to leave the country. Charles refused to move, so the astonished Sultan sent a regiment of troops to arrest him. When they appeared before Charles' house, he barricaded himself inside and fought off every attack until the Turks set fire to the building. Undaunted, Charles rushed out into the open and hurled himself upon the surprised Turks. Fortunately, before he suffered any serious injury, the Swedish King tripped over his long spurs and fell sprawling to the ground where the Turks overpowered him. Now that he had no choice but to leave Turkey, Charles wasted no time on his return journey. He was keen to get home in order to raise new armies with which to attack his enemies.

By this time, Peter had completed the conquest of the Baltic provinces and was invading Finland, meeting little resistance. For some time, he had been waiting for an opportunity to weaken Swedish sea power in the Baltic. This chance came in May 1714, when he learned that a Swedish fleet of sixteen ships-of-the-line, five frigates and many galleys was lying at anchor off Cape Hango in Finland. Hardly able to believe their luck, the Russians set sail with twenty ships-of-the-line and nearly two hundred galleys under the command of General-Admiral Apraxin and Rear-Admiral Peter Romanov!

On 26th July, Apraxin forced the Swedes to give battle and completely out-manoeuvred them. Although most of the Swedish fleet managed to slip away into the Baltic, some were forced to take refuge in Rilaks Fjord, where they were trapped by Peter. Knowing that the Swedish ships were better manned and armed

Opposite Russian galleys (in the foreground) defeat a Swedish fleet at the battle of Cape Hango.

than his own, Peter offered the Swedes fair terms of surrender, but these were contemptuously refused.

On 27th July Peter led his squadron, which outnumbered the Swedes by three to one, into the attack. Fortunately for the Russians, the fjord was so narrow that the Swedes were unable to make use of their superior seamanship. After a thunderous bombardment lasting three hours, Admiral Ehrenskjold struck his flag and the Swedes surrendered. Peter captured one frigate and nine galleys. He was overjoyed, and claimed that this victory was as great as that of Poltava. This was not true; Sweden's pride had been hurt, but she was still a naval power to be reckoned with. All the same, it was Russia's first naval victory and gave warning of her increasing efficiency and strength.

Meanwhile, the great struggle for the control of the Spanish empire was over, and the Western powers were able to take a keen interest in what was going on in the Baltic. They did not like what they saw. Most of them, especially George I of England, viewed Russia's rapid progress with alarm. In the following years, Peter and George waged a secret war against each other. George sent help to the Swedes and tried to persuade the Prussians, the Holy Roman Emperor and even the Cossacks to attack Russia. Peter for his part gave James Stuart, the Old Pretender, all the help he could, hoping that he would be able to regain the English throne. None of these schemes came to anything, however.

Disappointed by the slow progress of the war against Sweden, early in 1717 Peter decided to make another tour of Europe in search of allies to fight against Charles XII. This time, although he visited Germany and Holland, he spent most of his time in France. On reaching Paris, he refused to occupy the splendid suite of rooms that had been prepared for him in the Louvre (the residence of the French kings before Versailles had been built). Instead he insisted on going to live in an ordinary house. As soon as the welcoming ceremonies were over, he set off on an extensive tour of the French capital. He was particularly interested in the

Gobelins (the royal tapestry works), and the Mint, where he watched the craftsmen cast a medal with his image on it. However, the high point of his stay was his visit to the palace of Versailles, where he insisted on seeing Madame de Maintenon, Louis XIV's widow. When the frightened old lady refused to see him, he

Above Peter meets the seven-year-old Louis XV, King of France. Peter shocked the deferential French courtiers by holding the King in his arms.

forced his way into her private apartments, pulled back the curtains surrounding her bed, stared at her long and hard and then marched off without saying a word.

Peter was as unsuccessful in finding allies on his second European tour as he had been on his first. The Western powers feared that Russia was becoming too strong. They were afraid that if Peter finally defeated the Swedes and the Turks, he might turn westwards and upset the delicate balance of power between France, Britain, and Austria. As long as the war lasted, they were happy to give a little encouragement to both sides.

10 A Royal Tragedy

On his return to Russia, Peter found himself facing a major crisis caused by his eldest son, Alexis. Relations between father and son had never been good. Peter had taken Alexis away from his mother in 1698, and then paid no attention to him. Alexis was a sensitive boy who desperately needed love and affection. Deprived of these, he grew up to be a cold and suspicious man. Alexis' character was totally different from Peter's. Alexis was a sincere but narrow-minded member of the Orthodox Church, while Peter was happy to tolerate any religion that didn't interfere with the running of the country. Alexis was a conservative who hated the reforms his father was imposing upon the Russians. Peter desperately wanted his son to take an interest in his campaigns, but the Tsarevich showed no aptitude for either military or civil affairs.

In 1707 Peter divorced his wife Eudoxia and married his mistress, Catherine, who had been nothing more than a serving girl. Alexis felt that this was an insult to his mother, and made his disgust obvious. This was foolish, though quite understandable, because Catherine was a highly intelligent woman who provided Peter with just the kind of companionship he needed. The Tsar took her everywhere with him, even on campaign. Peter and Eudoxia, on the other hand, had never enjoyed one another's company.

Matters became infinitely worse when Peter forced his deeply religious son to marry Princess Charlotte of Brunswick-Wolfenbuttel in 1711. The unfortunate little German Princess was a Protestant, so Alexis felt that he was committing a mortal sin by living with her.

> "It is not work I want from you, but goodwill. I have thought well to address this appeal to you and wait a little longer to see if, perchance, you will turn from the error of your ways. If you do not, be quite sure that I will deprive you of the succession; I will cut you off as though you were a gangrenous swelling."
>
> *Peter writing to Alexis, 22nd October 1715.*

63

Above Peter sees his future wife Catherine for the first time.

"A shapeless body, monstrously fat, a head as big as a bushel measure, hairs growing on her face, sores on her legs . . . she is acute, subtle and shrewd in mind as she is broad, short and coarse in person." *Adrien de la Neuville writing about Peter's second wife Catherine.*

Peter was not interested in his son's religious objections: all he cared about was getting a male heir to the throne. Alexis made poor Charlotte's life a misery by his heavy drinking and unkindness. Finally, in 1715, the unhappy Princess died giving birth to a son named Peter. Curiously, only three weeks later, Peter's wife, Catherine, also gave birth to a son called Peter.

During this time, Alexis put himself at the head of the "Long Beards" who opposed his father's reforms. When Peter learned what his son was doing, he ordered him to conform, or else retire into a monastery. Alexis was so frightened that he agreed to everything, even recognizing his baby half-brother as heir to the throne. Peter, however, was still not satisfied, and ordered Alexis to join the army in Denmark or take his vows as a monk. Alexis was terrified into agreeing to join his father, but instead of going to Denmark as he had

Left Peter liked to be portrayed as a triumphant warrior in full armour, but in fact he wore everyday dress in battle.

promised, he fled first to Vienna and then to Naples.

Peter was furious at Alexis' disobedience, and ashamed at the disgrace to the family. He ordered his son to return. Understandably, Alexis was reluctant to agree until he was promised that he would not be punished. On reaching home on 31st February, 1718, Alexis went straight to his father and begged his forgiveness. Peter was touched, and for a moment it looked as if father and son would be reconciled. But by the next morning, the Tsar's heart had hardened and he had his son arrested, accused of treason and hauled before a special tribunal. The frightened Tsarevich was horribly tortured and forced to admit that he had several times wished his father dead; but he denied that he had ever plotted against him. Peter was not

"**The Tsarina has a stumpy little body, very brown, and had neither air nor grace . . . with her huddle of clothes she looked for all the world like a German playactress.**" *Description of Catherine by Frederick the Great of Prussia.*

satisfied, and had his son's friends arrested and tortured. Some died cruelly on the rack, some were beaten to death and some were beheaded. Even Alexis' mistress was forced to testify against him. The court's verdict was a foregone conclusion. Alexis was found guilty of treason and imprisoned in the grim castle of Peter and Paul on an island in the River Neva.

It was here that Peter and Alexis met for the last time. The Tsar crossed the river in the dead of night and had his son woken up. When the poor young man was told

Above A romantic nineteenth century view of Peter's meeting with his son Alexis on the latter's return from Italy.

Opposite Peter sailing on the River Neva with Catherine, his second wife. Notice the religious painting at the foot of the mast.

that he was to be executed, he collapsed. No one knows quite what happened to Alexis after that. Some said that he was smothered while he slept, others that he was beheaded, and still others that he was flogged to death. All that we know for certain is that his death was announced on 7th July 1718.

As if in punishment for his callous treatment of his eldest child, Peter's second and favourite son, Peter Petrovich, died in May 1719, and although Catherine bore Peter another son in 1723, he too died immediately. Russia was thus without a male heir to the throne. This was a serious matter, since it meant that when Peter died there might be a civil war over who should succeed him. True, he had two attractive and talented daughters, Anne and Elizabeth, but Russia needed sons and in this respect if in no other, Peter failed his country.

11 Peter's Triumph

IN 1718, CHARLES XII WAS KILLED while besieging a Norwegian castle. When his body was examined, it was found that he had been shot through the back of the head. Perhaps he was murdered by one of his own war-weary soldiers. For a time it looked as if the Swedes would make peace, but their new King, Frederick of Hesse-Cassel, hoped to regain some of the lost provinces of the Swedish empire with the help of the western powers.

George I of England was eager to help Frederick, but did not dare to declare war on Peter because of the Tsar's friendship with the powerful British merchants who traded with Russia. Instead, he sent a British fleet to the Baltic with secret orders to destroy the Russian navy. Fortunately, Peter guessed what George was up to, and attacked and destroyed the Swedish fleet before the British arrived. Then, the Russians emphasized their naval superiority by raiding the Swedish mainland. This disaster convinced Frederick that there was no point in prolonging the war, and he sued for peace. By the Treaty of Nystadt in 1721, the Russians retained control of Ingria, Estonia, Livonia and Karelia on the eastern coast of the Baltic. They returned most of Finland to Sweden, and paid a large indemnity to compensate her for the loss of most of her empire. Thus, after twenty-one years of hard fighting, Russia succeeded in replacing Sweden as the greatest power in the Baltic area.

The new Baltic provinces of the Russian empire needed very careful handling. The Balts were very different people from the Russians. They spoke

"A ball weighing half-a-pound had struck him on the right temple, leaving a hole large enough to turn three fingers in, his head had fallen over the parapet, his left eye was driven in and his right out of its socket." *The Swedish official statement on the death of Charles XII.*

different languages, they had their own customs and traditions, and they were mostly Protestants. Peter was careful not to upset them. He angered the Russian nobility by refusing to let them acquire estates in the new provinces. Instead, he left the government of the area in the hands of the German squires and merchants who dominated it since the Middle Ages. Thanks to this wise policy, Peter never had any trouble with the Balts. On the contrary, they became some of his most loyal subjects.

No sooner had the Treaty of Nystadt been signed than Peter, seeking new conquests, declared war on the Persian Empire. The Tsar was anxious to gain possession of the famous silk manufacturing areas along the coast of the Caspian Sea. Peter led his armies in person and inflicted one defeat after another upon the unfortunate Persians until the Shah was forced to beg for peace. The Shah handed over the western and southern coasts of the Caspian to the victorious Russians. However, this was the last of Peter's military successes. His armies were defeated when they clashed with the Turks for a third time, and Peter had to recognize the Sultan as ruler of Azerbaijan, Armenia and Georgia, areas which he had hoped to gain for Russia.

Throughout Peter's reign, the Russians penetrated deeper and deeper into Siberia. The Tsar hoped and believed that the Central Asian *steppes* were rich in minerals, particularly gold. Four large expeditions explored the area between 1714 and 1722, but without making any startling discoveries. In the meantime, more and more Russian settlers arrived and carved rich farms out of the grasslands. Frontier towns like Omsk, founded in 1717, sprang up to supply the needs of the growing population. The new towns were very like the early settlements in America. Their people were a curious mixture of settlers, prospectors, fur traders, convicts, and nomads. The native peoples of the area, the Tartars, Yakuts and Kazakhs, feared the advance of the Russians like the Indians feared that of the

"Siberia is the place whither the Czar banishes capital criminals and offenders, never to return." *Captain John Perry, The State of Russia.*

Opposite A symbolic engraving displaying Peter's achievements in the fields of war, commerce, planning and administration.

Above Ritzart Island and the mouth of the River Neva in 1706. The farm on the right marks the future site of Kronstadt, and the first buildings of St. Petersburg can be seen in the distance.

Opposite A map of the north coast of Russia drawn by William Barents in 1598. The area was again explored during Peter's reign by Vitus Behring, but no sea route to the Pacific could be found.

American colonists. Life on the Russian frontier was as tough as that in the Wild West. The Tsar's agents found it almost impossible to maintain law and order or to collect taxes. If the frontiersmen did not like life in the new settlements, they just packed up and disappeared into the wilderness.

Peter was as keen to build up Russia's trade with the rest of the world as he was to add to his empire. When he conquered the Baltic provinces with their great ports of Riga and Reval, he hoped to build up a profitable trade with Western Europe. Russia already exported thousands of tons of natural products – one list written at the time mentions furs, hemp, flax, hides, tallow, honey, wax, bristles, caviar, sealskins, whale oil, timber, resin, pitch, tar and ash, in order of importance. However, it was the English and Dutch merchants, who carried on this trade, who made the most money out of it. Peter was determined to get a share in this profitable commerce for the Russian state, but he always remained dependant on the British and Dutch for good

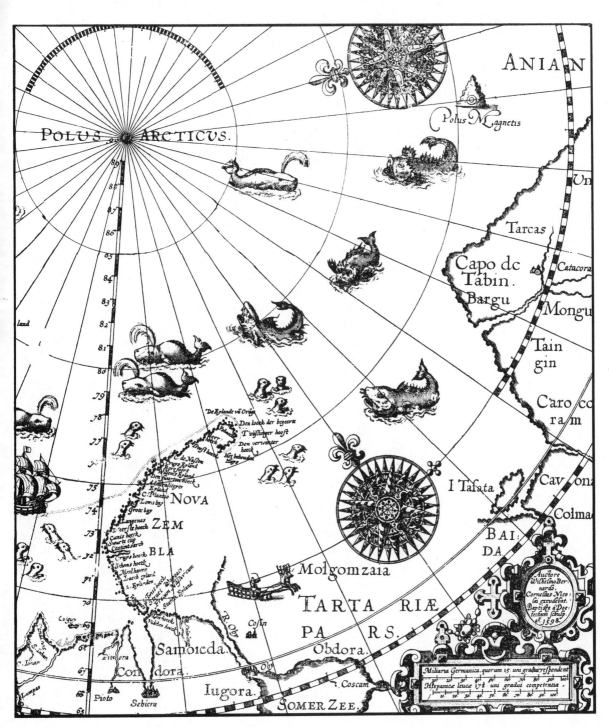

ANIAN

POLVS ARCTICVS.

Polus Magnetis

Tarcas

Capo de
Tabin.
Bargu

Mongu

Tain
gin

Caro co
ra m

Cav ona

Colma

I Tafata

BAI
DA.

Auctore
Wilhi Gno Ber
nardo,
Cornelius Nico
lai excudebat.
Baptista d'Doe
techum sculp:
a° 1598.

De Eylande va Orige
Den hoeck der begeert
T'vislinger hooft
Den verwinter
hoeck
Het behouden
Huys

C. de Nassou
Langa Eyland
Barents fort
Willem Eyland
S. swarten hoeck
Admiralteyts
Eyland
C. Plance
Lombsby
Groote bay
Langenes
D'eerste hoeck
Canis hoeck
Swarte clip
Costin sarch
Cruys hoeck
Schans hoeck
Meerl hauen
Lacch eyland
2. Eylanden
Staten hoeck
Sweer Wolthais
Kerens Wolfhairen
Staten Eyland

NOVA
ZEM
BLA

Molgomzaia

TARTA RIÆ
PA RS.
Obdora.

R.Oby

Cofin

R.Oby

Oby

Coscam

Samoieda.
Con dora.
Iugora.

Pioto
Sebiera

SOMER ZEE.

Miliaria Germanica, quorum 15. uni gradui respondent
Hispanice leuce 17¼ uni gradui competentia

D

ships and trained seamen. His attempt to create a merchant navy ended in dismal failure.

Now that his hopes of a great European market were dashed, Peter turned to Asia. For many years, he hoped to develop a flourishing trade with India. Several Russian expeditions made their way overland to India, but the journey through Turkestan and across the Himalaya Mountains was far too hazardous to become a regular trade route. In 1723, Peter ordered two of his warships to sail from the Baltic to Madagascar, an island off the coast of South Africa. Their mission was to set up a naval base on the island where Russian ships could stop and refit before continuing their voyages to India. This attempt failed when one of the ships sprang a leak and the expedition had to be abandoned before it had left the Baltic.

China, too, was a potentially rich market. Unfortunately, the Russians and Chinese had been struggling for possession of the rich valley of the River Amur for years before Peter came to the throne. However, in 1689, the Russians signed the Treaty of Nerchinsk and withdrew from the Amur region. As a result Russo-Chinese relations grew warmer, and after 1696 caravans became a common sight on the road between Moscow and Peking.

Another of Peter's dreams was to find a passage from Western Europe to China and India through the ice of the Arctic Ocean. With this in mind, he sent Vitus Behring to explore the area to the north of Kamchatka. During this famous voyage, the great explorer discovered the straits between Russia and America. A few years after Peter's death, a number of Russians crossed the straits and founded a colony in Alaska.

Peter's expansionist policies thus met with mixed success. True, he had conquered the Baltic provinces, and taken over large areas of Siberia. All the same, he failed to make Russia a great trading nation.

12 Reform

PETER'S REPEATED WARS put an intolerable strain upon Russia's antiquated system of government. The Tsar realized that if Russia was to become a great power the whole structure would have to be rebuilt. He had no overall plan for reform, and dealt with problems as they arose. As a result, many of his solutions were short-term ones which had to be modified later. Nevertheless, by means of trial and error, he gradually improved the administration.

After a time, it became clear that Peter needed a special organization to rule Russia while he was away on campaign. He therefore created the Senate. This council of nine ministers became a kind of "think-tank" to help the Tsar with all aspects of policy-making and government. Next, it was obvious that the old departments of state, the *prikasy* would have to go, and be replaced by more efficient bodies, each specializing in one aspect of government and dealing with the whole of Russia. Seven "Colleges" were therefore set up to deal with finance, commerce, mines and manufactures, foreign affairs, the army, navy, and justice. These Colleges were supervised by the Procurator-General and a number of "fiscals," who checked up on the civil servants and reported any abuses. They became the best-hated men in Russia.

During the same period, Peter tried several times to strengthen the local government service, but without much success. In 1708, he divided Russia into eight *Gubernia* or provinces, but their governors found that they were far too large to control. In 1719, Peter scrapped this system and divided Russia into fifty

"There cannot be good administration except with Colleges: their mechanism is like that of watches, whose wheels mutually keep each other in movement." *Gottfried Leibniz, the mathematician and philosopher, speaking to Peter.*

provinces on the Swedish model. But this did not work well, either. Now there were far too many local authorities; the cost was ruinous, and the results inefficient.

At the same time, Peter tried to streamline the Russian system of justice by separating it from the administration. Each provice was provided with judges from the College of Justice, so that there would be no corruption. However, within a few years of Peter's death, the courts were staffed once again by the local people, and so they became as corrupt and unfair as their predecessors. No real progress was made in this aspect of government until the nineteenth century.

Although Peter was a loyal member of the Orthodox Church, he was tolerant of all other religions. He let Protestants and Roman Catholics in his new provinces worship God as they pleased. This infuriated the more bigoted of his Orthodox subjects. He even refused to persecute the "Old Believers," because, as he said, "If reason cannot turn them from their superstition, neither fire nor sword can do so. It is foolish to make them martyrs." This was not to the liking of most of his bishops and priests. As Peter's reign went on, they became more and more critical, not only of his religious policy but of his reforms in general. This opposition had to be stopped. In 1700, when the Patriarch, the head of the Russian Orthodox Church, died, Peter refused to appoint a successor and instead set up a commission to rule the Church. This experiment worked so well that the Tsar set up a special new department – the Holy Governing Synod – to carry out the functions of the Patriarch. This new body was organized just like the other Colleges. As a result, the Orthodox Church became the most loyal supporter of the monarchy.

Peter was desperately short of money throughout his reign. He taxed almost everything he could think of: beards, coffins, tobacco, baths, beehives, melons, cellars, chimney stacks and firewood. In spite of all these taxes, however, the Treasury remained depres-

76

singly empty. In his search for money, Peter forced the Church to advance large sums to help finance his wars, but this was only a short term solution to his problems. What he needed was a revolutionary new tax which would raise large sums and yet be easy to collect. At last, his advisers thought they had found such a tax. In 1718, it was announced that every male in Russia, except the clergy and nobility, was to pay a levy of seventy-four kopeks per head. This "Poll tax," as it was called, was a disaster. The peasants were already grossly overtaxed, and many of them fled to the frontier lands rather than take on yet another burden. Moreover, even this tax failed to solve the Tsar's financial problems. In fact, nothing could be done as long as the nobility and clergy, who owned most of the nation's wealth, weren't made to pay anything towards the cost

Above Peter talks with Russian and foreign merchants on the Bourse (trading exchange) at Archangel, Russia's northern port.

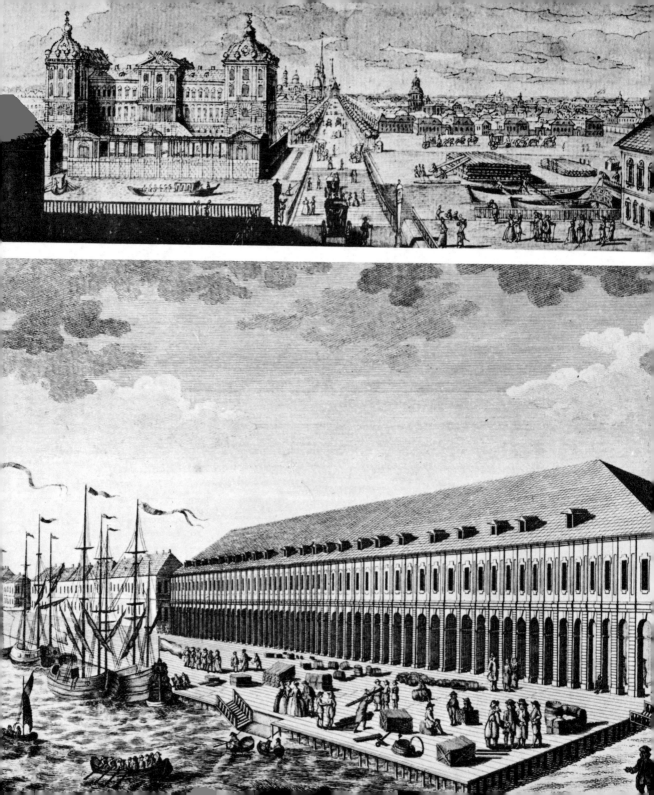

of the government.

His frequent wars also forced Peter to encourage Russia's new industries. The army and navy needed cannon, muskets and gunpowder, so an armaments industry was created. As the soldiers and sailors needed uniforms, the textile industry was reorganized to make better-quality cloth. The rise of the Russian navy stimulated the growth of rope, sail and timber manufacture. At first, Peter had to get together most of the capital and workers for these new industries. Once the Great Northern War was over, however, he was able to hand over many of these projects to private individuals. The last part of his reign saw the rise of a number of luxury industries. China, glass, silk and velvet were produced for those who could afford them. However, on Peter's death, many of these enterprises collapsed through lack of money and government support.

Peter may not have dared to tax the nobility, but he could – and did – make them serve their country. From the beginning of his reign, he forced them to enter either the armed forces or the civil service. In 1722, he went further and set up "the Table of Ranks." The senior posts in the armed forces and the civil service were divided into fourteen ranks, and it was announced that no one would be allowed to enjoy the privileges of nobility until they had worked their way up to one of these ranks. In effect, this meant that anybody could become a noble if they had enough ability. Naturally enough, the old nobility hated this system and it was discontinued when Peter died.

As Peter was anxious to prevent the break-up of the great estates, he changed the laws of inheritance. Under the old law, estates had been divided up between all the sons of a landowner on his death. Now, the eldest son was to receive everything. In this way, the Tsar replaced a large number of petty nobles by a small class of great ones.

Among all his other activities, Peter found time to create more educational opportunities in Russia. In

> "I will persuade my idle priests to cultivate the garden and plots so that they will be assured of their daily bread, and will lead a better life." *Peter the Great.*

Opposite Two views of the quays and warehouses of St. Petersburg shortly after Peter's death. Timber and other goods are being unloaded.

79

"His Piety is visible in his noble Attempt to reform the Manners of his People, his Resolution great in thwarting their Inclinations, obliging them to relinquish their long-espoused Errors and superstitious Practices which they were born and bred in." *T. Consett, The Present State and Regulations of the Church of Russia (1729).*

Left Peter, in classical costume, is shown offering the benefits of education and technology to a representative of the old Russia.

1714, he insisted that Cyphering Schools should be set up in every province to teach the nobility to read and write. Over forty schools of this type were opened during Peter's reign, but they could never educate more than five hundred children at a time. In 1721, Peter tried to provide education for the children of the professional classes, by insisting that there should be schools in each diocese for the children of the clergy and that garrison schools should be opened to educate the children of soldiers and sailors. Russia was still without a university, so Peter founded the Russian Academy of Sciences, opened in 1724 for students studying mathematics, physics and other useful subjects for soldiers. Yet in spite of all his efforts, the huge majority of Russians were still illiterate at the end of his reign.

Although there was only a small reading public in Russia, Peter published an official newsheet called the *Vedomosti*. Admittedly it only appeared at irregular intervals, but it was a beginning. As he grew older, Peter became more and more interested in the arts. He tried hard to encourage the growth of a Russian theatre, but its audiences were restricted to members of the noble classes. In 1716, he began buying paintings in Amsterdam. Two years later, he was buying statues and paintings in Rome and hiring Italian sculptors and artists to work in Russia, For the first time, there were visible signs of Western influence in Russian art and architecture. In accordance with the fashion for imitating Greek and Roman models, columns, porticos and entablatures began to appear upon the houses of the rich. Russian painters began to introduce realism into their paintings, and to borrow ideas from the great French landscape painters such as Poussin and Claude.

Without doubt, this second phase of Peter's reign saw the crumbling of many traditional Russian attitudes and beliefs, mainly among the noble classes. It was to be many years before these changes were accepted by the middle classes, let alone by the ordinary people. The huge majority of Russians remained as hostile to change as they had been before Peter came to the throne.

"The Czar pulls uphill with the strength of ten, but millions pull downhill. How then can his work prevail?" *Peasant Pososhkov.*

81

13 The Achievements of Peter the Great

By 1724, Peter was a sick man of fifty-two, suffering from kidney stones and venereal disease. During his last years, his fits of violent temper became more and more frequent. On these occasions, his second wife Catherine was the only person who could do anything with him. She would cradle his head in her lap and stroke his forehead for hours on end until the pain disappeared.

Then, one day in mid-November 1724, the Tsar came across some shipwrecked sailors struggling in the icy waters of a canal. Without stopping to think, he dived into the canal and helped to rescue them. As a result, he was chilled to the bone and developed a raging fever. On 28th January 1725, Peter the Great died.

The official statements expressed the admiration which many people had felt for him, but in his last years he had come to be hated for his brutal dictatorship and terrifying rages. The news of his death was greeted with relief throughout Russia and the rest of Europe.

How great an effect did Peter have upon Russia? When he came to the throne, Russia was an insignificant state. He made it into a great power feared by all. At his accession Russia had no armed forces except for the inefficient and untrustworthy Streltsy. When he died, there was a professional army of 210,000 men. He created a navy out of nothing, leaving behind him a fleet of forty-eight ships-of-the-line and many smaller vessels.

His reign had been one of continuous territorial expansion. He had conquered the Baltic Provinces and the western shores of the Caspian, but had failed to realize his hopes of gaining access to the Black Sea and adding Azerbaijan, Armenia and Georgia to his empire. Vast areas of Siberia had been occupied in his name.

Peter had brought about deep and lasting changes in Russian society. He had created an hereditary nobility who owed their position to the monarchy and therefore tended to support it. The ignorance and conservatism of this class was greatly weakened. In many cases, their selfish ambitions were replaced by the ideal of service to the state. In much the same way, the clergy of the Russian Orthodox Church ceased being the bitterest critics of the monarchy and became its most faithful supporters. This was not without its dangers. It was Peter's unwillingness to offend the nobility and clergy by taxing their vast wealth that made it impossible for him to gain the loyalty of the common people and carry out many other necessary reforms.

Peter signally failed to create the large, thriving middle class that Russia needed. In spite of the most strenuous efforts, Russia's commerce and industry remained dependent upon the Tsar, so that when he died, there were not enough wealthy, far-sighted traders and industrialists to develop what he had begun. This lack of private initiative and enterprise was to remain one of Russia's greatest social weaknesses until the Communist Revolution of 1917.

From the point of view of the Russian peasant, Peter's reign was a total disaster. During this period, most of them lost their freedom and became serfs, who could be bought and sold at their master's pleasure. Thousands were dragged from their homes and put to work in the new shipyards and ironworks. Thousands more perished helping to build St. Petersburg. The strongest and fittest of their young men were forced to serve in the Tsar's army and navy. Heavy taxes made it impossible for them to save enough money to escape from poverty. In the end it was more than flesh and blood could stand, and the peasants rose in revolt all over Russia.

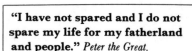

"I have not spared and I do not spare my life for my fatherland and people." *Peter the Great.*

Left *The Mice Bury the Dead Cat* This popular cartoon shows the Russians playing bagpipes, drums and horns to celebrate the death of the Tsar they had feared and respected. Notice that the cat still clutches a dead mouse between its jaws – and that one of the mice holds a whip to encourage the unwilling workers.

But such was the power and wealth of the Tsar and the nobility that they were always defeated. In spite of all their efforts, the Russian serfs were not granted their freedom until 1861.

Peter's valiant attempts to improve Russia's ailing economy also met with mixed success. Russia remained a producer of raw materials for the world market. She exported thousands of tons of hemp and timber products, but not in her own ships. Her efforts to build up her own industries were frustrated by shortages of skilled men, capital and good management. Her hopes of increasing her trade in Europe were thwarted by the all-powerful British and Dutch merchants. Although new markets were won in India and China, they were too small to make any real difference. As a result, Russia developed as an industrial and trading nation much more slowly than the rest of Europe until the second half of the nineteenth century.

In the world of education and the arts, Peter faced similar difficulties. When he came to the throne, neither the desire nor the means existed to provide even the nobility with an elementary education. Many schools were founded during Peter's reign, but they still lacked competent teachers and textbooks. Many years were to pass before the Russians could fill these gaps. Significantly, the Tsar did manage to awaken an interest in the arts and sciences among the nobility and middle classes. By the nineteenth century, novelists like Leo Tolstoy and scientists such as Pavlov were leaders in their fields. Peter drew Russia out of her medieval isolation and into the mainstream of European culture.

It would be a mistake to imagine that Peter the Great transformed medieval Muscovy into modern Russia. Carrying on where his father Alexis and before him Ivan the Terrible had left off, he greatly speeded up the rate at which changes were taking place in Russia. In many ways he was far in advance of his time, and many of his hopes and ambitions were not realized for several generations. So much of what he had done depended on his own force of character, and it was too

easy for things to slip back when a weaker or lazier Tsar was in charge.

Why was Peter able to achieve as much as he did? Like all great rulers, Peter identified himself with his homeland. He lived for his country and believed that his interests and Russia's were one and the same. He had boundless energy and determination and refused to be dismayed by setbacks in either civil or military affairs. He worked hard and long and always set a magnificent personal example. As a soldier, he fought with his men in the front line of the battle. As a shipbuilder, he was prepared to strip off his coat and work side by side with his own men. This huge capacity for work won him the admiration of all.

Above Peter's achievements as a conqueror are celebrated in this print. Behind him are plans of the fortresses he captured.

Although Peter was never an original thinker, he was able to recognize ability in others and to use their ideas. Throughout his life, he was always ready to learn from others. He had physical and moral courage. He was ready to meet his enemies in battle, and to go in the face of all accepted opinion – a much more difficult thing. Moreover, he was able to inspire others with his vision of a new and greater Russia.

Of course, he had weaknesses as well as strengths. His rashness sometimes placed him in difficulties, as when he attacked Turkey in 1711 without planning his campaign in sufficient detail. He could be unbelievably cruel, as was shown by his persecution of his unfortunate wife and son, Eudoxia and Alexis. He lacked respect for people who thought differently from himself and ridiculed them mercilessly in the Drunken Association of Fools. His desperate energy made him coarse and insensitive – he felt he could not afford to be kind and considerate.

Nevertheless, he was "every inch a king." He towered above his contemporaries not only in size but in belief and dedication. He spared neither himself nor anybody else in his determination to create a better Russia. In his weaknesses and in his strengths, he was a giant among men, and fully deserves the proud title of "Peter the Great."

Opposite Peter was never a popular man during his lifetime, but after his death he came to be seen as a heroic figure, and was a favourite subject for historical painters. Here he is seen, in his usual commanding pose, superintending the work on the first buildings of St. Petersburg.

Table of Dates

1645–76   Tsar Alexis wins the support of the Zarporogian Cossacks, and puts down the rising of Stenka Razin.

1672   Birth of Peter, son of Alexis and his second wife Natalia Naryshkina.

1676–82   Fedor II, the sickly eldest son of Alexis, succeeds but dies early leaving an equally sickly younger brother, Ivan, as heir to the throne.

1682   Peter I (the Great) elected Tsar. Sophia Miloslavsky forces the election of Ivan V as co-Tsar.

1682–89   Sophia is Regent for both boy Tsars. Peter is hidden away in Preobrazhensk.

1689   Sophia tries to have Peter murdered, but he escapes.

1689–94   Regency of Natalia Naryshkina.

1689   Peter marries Eudoxia Lopukhina.

1690   Birth of the Tsarevich Alexis.

1694   Death of Natalia Naryshkina. Peter begins to rule.

1695–1700   Russo-Turkish War.

1696   Peter captures Azoff.

1697–98   The Grand Embassy. Peter visits Latvia, Germany, Holland, England, and the Holy Roman Empire.

1698   The Streltsy rise in revolt and Peter has to return home. Eudoxia is forced to enter a convent.

1699   Secret alliance between Russia and Poland against Sweden.

1700	Peter introduces Western clothes into Russia.
1700–21	The Great Northern War between Sweden and Denmark, Poland and Russia begins.
1700	Charles XII of Sweden defeats Peter at the battle of Narva.
1701–02	The Russians occupy Livonia and Estonia.
1703	Peter issues Russia's first newspaper, the *Vedomosti*.
1704	Peter invades Ingria and captures Narva. He starts to build St. Petersburg.
1707	Konrad Bulavin and the Don Cossacks lead a great peasant uprising in southern Russia.
1708	Peter divorces Eudoxia and secretly marries Catherine, Charles XII invades the Ukraine.
1709	Russia is divided into eight *Gubernia*.
1709	The Battle of Poltava. Peter destroys Charles' army but Charles escapes to Turkey.
1711–12	The Second Russo-Turkish War. The Russian army is surrounded by the Turks near the River Pruth. Peter makes peace.
1711	The Senate is set up.
1712	Peter officially marries Catherine.
1713	St. Petersburg replaces Moscow as capital of Russia.
1713–14	Peter conquers Finland.
1714	The Battle of Cape Hango. The Russians defeat the Swedes for the first time at sea.
	Peter insists that all members of the nobility serve in the armed forces or the civil service.
1716	The Tsarevich Alexis flees to Vienna and then Naples.
1717	Peter tours Europe for the second time but cannot find any new allies.
1718	Alexis returns, is tried, and executed. The Poll Tax is introduced.

	Charles XII of Sweden is shot dead in Norway.
1719	Russia is divided up into fifty provinces.
1720	The old *Prikasy* are replaced by seven Colleges and the Procurator-General is appointed.
	The Swedes are heavily defeated at sea, and the Swedish mainland is raided by Russian fleets.
1721	The Treaty of Nystadt brings the Great Northern War to an end and confirms Russia in possession of the Baltic States and part of Finland.
	The Holy Governing Synod is set up to rule the Russian Church instead of the Patriarch.
1722–24	The Russo-Persian War. Peter leads his army to the Caspian and conquers the western and southern coasts.
1722–24	The Third Russo-Turkish War. The Russians are defeated and Peter has to recognize the Sultan as ruler of Azerbaijan, Armenia and Georgia.
1722	The Garrison Schools are opened. The "Table of Ranks" is introduced.
1723	Unsuccessful attempt to send fleet to Madagascar to open a naval base for trading with India.
1724	Catherine, Peter's second wife, is crowned Empress. Peter develops a fatal chill after helping to save some sailors from drowning in an icy canal near St. Petersburg.
1725	Peter dies (28th January) and is succeeded by his widow, who becomes Catherine I (1725–27).

Principal Characters

ALEXIS I (1629–76), Tsar of Russia 1645–76, Peter the Great's father. He was a strong Tsar who won the support of the Zaporogian Cossacks and crushed the revolt led by Stenka Razin. He began the policy of Westernization which Peter was later to carry on.

ALEXIS (1690–1718), Tsarevich, Peter's eldest son. He was taken from his mother Eudoxia in 1698 and had a lonely and unhappy childhood. He went on the Narva campaign in 1704, but showed no interest in war or in government. In 1711 Peter forced him to marry Charlotte of Brunswick-Wolfenbuttel, a Protestant, despite Alexis's religious principles. He supported the Old Believers, and intrigued with Peter's enemies among the nobles. In 1716 Alexis fled from Russia, and on his return two years later, he was tried for treason and (probably) secretly executed.

CATHERINE I (1680–1727), Empress of Russia 1725–27. Catherine was the servant of a Lutheran pastor until she became Peter's mistress. They married secretly in 1707 and officially in 1712. Peter found her much more of a companion than he had Eudoxia, and she used to join him on his campaigns. She bore four sons and six daughters, but only two girls survived. She was popular at court, and was made Empress by the Guards on Peter's death.

CHARLES XII (1682–1718), King of Sweden 1697–1718. Charles was a brilliant general, obsessed by the desire for glory. He defeated the Danes, Poles and Russians while still in his teens, and kept eastern Europe at war throughout his reign. From 1709 to 1713, he

Right Charles XII of Sweden shortly before his death. Compare this with the magnificent portrait on p. 39 of him as a young man.

stayed in Turkey, refusing to leave his house until expelled by the Sultan. He died from a shot in the back of the head, perhaps fired by a discontented soldier.

EUDOXIA LOPUKHIN (168?–1731). Peter married Eudoxia against his will in 1689, and from the start ignored her and was unfaithful to her. Alexis, her son, was taken from her in 1698, when she was forced to enter a convent. Peter divorced her in 1707, but continued to persecute her, fearing that she might become a focus for opposition.

COUNT ALEXANDER MENSCHIKOV (1672–1729). Menschikov was selling cakes on the streets of Moscow when he first came to Peter's notice. He soon became a member of the Drunken Association of Fools and a general in Peter's army. He distinguished himself against the Swedes in 1704 and the Cossacks in 1708, and played a leading part at Poltava. Catherine, Peter's second wife, was a captive of his on the Baltic campaign, whom he later introduced to Peter. He fell from favour because of his corruption and extortion, but after Peter's death he became Catherine's chief minister. He was banished to Siberia in 1727.

SOPHIA MILOSLAVSKY (16??–1704). Daughter of Tsar Alexis by his first wife, she ruled as Regent for Peter and Ivan V from 1682 to 1689. In that year she tried to have Peter murdered, and when he escaped she was forced to take refuge in a nunnery. In 1698 she intrigued with the Streltsy to try to overthrow Peter, and for the rest of her life was kept as a virtual prisoner.

NATALIA NARYSHKINA (16??–1694). Second wife of Tsar Alexis and mother of Peter the Great. She was ambitious for her son, and in 1682 forced the Miloslavskys to accept Peter as co-Tsar. When Sophia sought revenge, she took Peter to Preobrazhensk for safety. She was effective ruler of Russia from 1689–1694.

Further Reading

The best simple accounts of the whole of Russian history are Richard Charques' *A Short History of Russia* (E.U.P., (1959), and Henry Moscow's *Russia and the Tsars* (Cassell, 1964). The latter contains many beautiful illustrations.

There are also some excellent books on the Romanov family. E. Almedingen's *The Romanovs* (The Bodley Head, 1966) is suitable for 11 to 16 year-olds. Virginia Cowles's *The Romanovs* (Collins, 1971) is aimed at older readers but is also very suitable for secondary school students.

Amongst the many biographies of Peter the Great, a few call for special mention:

Giancarlo Buzzi, *The Life and Times of Peter the Great* (Hamlyn, 1968) is a short, easy-to-read introduction with excellent illustrations.

Ian Grey, *Peter the Great* (Lippincott, 1960) is a thorough biography by an expert on Russian history.

Joan Joseph, *Peter the Great* (Julian Messner, 1968) is entertainingly written for secondary school readers.

V. Klyuchevsky, *Peter the Great*, translated L. Archibald (Macmillan, 1965) is much more difficult but was written by one of Russia's finest historians.

B. H. Sumner, *Peter the Great and the Emergence of Russia* (E.U.P., 1950) is probably the best all-round biography for 11 to 18 year-olds.

Index

Agriculture, 19
Alexis I, Tsar, 9, 31, 32, 86, 93
Alexis, Tsarevich, 24, 63–68, 89, 93
Archangel, port of, 10, 42
Army, 16, 23, 82
Art and Architecture, 81, 86
Artillery, 39
Autocracy, 8, 15
Azoff, port of, 26, 47, 51, 57

Baltic Provinces, 39, 57, 69, 72, 74, 82
Beards, 33
Behring, 74
Black Sea, 11, 24, 37, 57, 83
Bulavin, Konrad, 47
Boyars, 16
Byzantine Empire, 10, 11

Catherine I of Russia, 45, 63–5, 68, 82, 93
Cavalry, 16, 37, 49
Charles II of Spain, 12
Charles XII of Sweden, 37–9, 47–55, 57, 69, 93–4
Charlotte of Brunswick, 63, 64
China, relations with, 74, 86
"Colleges," 75
Cossacks, 9, 10, 38, 47–51, 60
Court, 44–6
Cyphering Schools, 81

Denmark, 10, 37, 64
Dress, 20, 33
Drinking, 18, 19, 25, 45
Drunken Association of Fools, 7, 26, 89

Education, 22, 33, 34, 79–81, 86
England, 27–9
Entertainment, 17, 81
Eudoxia Lopukhina, 24, 30, 31, 63, 89, 94
Evelyn, John, 27–8

Fedor I, Tsar, 9
Fedor II, Tsar, 21
Finland, 59, 69
France, 29, 60, 61

George I, King of England, 60
German Suburb of Moscow, 21
Godunov, Boris, Tsar, 9
Great Embassy, 27–29, 30
Great Northern War, 47
Gubernia, 75

Hango, battle of Cape, 59, 60
Holland, 12, 27, 41
Holy Governing Synod, 76
Holy Roman Empire, 11, 60
Huns, 7

India, 74, 86
Industry, 34, 79
Infantry, 37, 53
Ingria, 39, 41, 69
Ivan III, Tsar, 8, 9
Ivan IV, Tsar, 8, 86
Ivan V, Tsar, 21

James Stuart, 60

Latvia, 39, 69
Law and order, 76
Leopold I, Holy Roman Emperor, 12, 25
Lesnaya, Battle of, 51
Lesczynski, Stanislas, 37
Local government, 15, 75, 76
Louis XIV, 12, 13, 43

Madagascar, 74
Maintenon, Mme de, 61–2
Maria Miloslavsky, 21
Mazeppa, Ivan, 47–51
Menshikov, Alexander, 50–55, 94
Michael Romanov, Tsar, 9
Middle classes, 17, 18, 83
Mongols, 8, 17
Mons, Anna, 25
Moscow, 7, 17, 21, 26, 37, 41

Natalia Naryshkin, 21, 25, 94
Narva, battle of, 37
Navy, 24, 25, 34, 35, 59, 60, 82

Nobility, 16, 17, 34, 41, 77, 79
Novgorod, 51
Nystadt, treaty of, 69–71

Old Believers, 19, 30, 76
Omsk, 71
Orthodox Church, 7, 17, 26, 63, 76, 83
Ottoman Turks, 10, 11, 12, 17, 24, 25, 27, 29, 37, 52, 57–9, 89

Paris, 60, 61
Persia, 71
Poland, 10, 11, 37, 40, 47
Poll tax, 77
Poltava, battle of, 47–55, 57, 60
Prikasy, 15, 75
Procurator-General, 75
Prussia, 27, 60
Pruth campaign, 57–9

Senate, 75
Serfs, 19, 20, 83–6
Siberia, 12, 20, 71, 74, 83
Sophia Miloslavsky, Tsarevna, 21, 25, 30, 31, 94
St Petersburg, 41–4, 55, 83, 89
Steppes, 12, 71, 72
Streltsy, 15, 16, 21, 30, 31, 82

Table of Ranks, 79
Taxation, 15, 76–79, 83
"Time of Troubles," 9
Tobacco, 35
Town life, 17
Trade, 17, 72, 83–6

Ukraine, 10, 50
Ural mountains, 34

Varangian Vikings, 7
Vasily III, Tsar 9

Westernization, 34, 35, 75
William III, King of England, 12, 27
Women, Russian, 17

Picture Credits

The author and publishers wish to thank the following for their kind permission to reproduce copyright illustrations which appear on the pages mentioned: Radio Times Hulton Picture Library, *frontispiece*, 9, 31, 33, 36, 39, 42, 43, 46, 48–9, 56, 66, 78 *top & bottom*, 84–5, 88; Mansell Collection, *jacket back*, 6, 10, 16, 22, 23, 35, 64, 65, 67; Mary Evans Picture Library, 8 *right*, 23, 26, 30, 34, 70, 72, 93; Royal Holloway College, *jacket front*; Bulloz, Paris, 13; Novosti Press Agency, 28, 52. The remaining pictures are the property of the Wayland Picture Library.